Presented To:

_____

From:

_____

Date:

_____

SEEING THROUGH
HEAVEN'S EYES

SEEING THROUGH HEAVEN'S EYES

A World View That Will
TRANSFORM YOUR LIFE

LEIF HETLAND

DESTINY IMAGE. PUBLISHERS, INC.
P.O. Box 310, Shippensburg, PA 17257-0310

"Speaking to the Purposes of God for This Generation and for the Generations to Come."

This book and all other Destiny Image, Revival Press, MercyPlace, Fresh Bread, Destiny Image Fiction, and Treasure House books are available at Christian bookstores and distributors worldwide.

For a U.S. bookstore nearest you, call 1-800-722-6774.
For more information on foreign distributors, call 717-532-3040.
Reach us on the Internet: www.destinyimage.com.

ISBN 13 TP: 978-0-7684-4014-0
ISBN 13 Ebook: 978-0-7684-8928-6

For Worldwide Distribution, Printed in the U.S.A.
3 4 5 6 7 8 9 10 11 / 13

DEDICATION

I want to dedicate this book to my parents, Sven and Laila Hetland. Thank you for seeing me through Heaven's eyes.

ACKNOWLEDGMENTS

You don't write a book without a lot of help from a lot of people who have influenced you throughout your life. Some were particularly influential.

Jennifer, my beloved wife and best friend, you are my biggest cheerleader and the most beautiful and valuable person in my life.

Leif Emmanuel, Laila, Courtney, and Katherine, you make my life richer for knowing you. I am proud to be your father and excited to see you become world changers.

To my board members: Papa Jack, you have given me a godly inheritance. Your patience and kindness are endless! Rick and Bob, you guys really know how to put this Norwegian in a great place. Your support is invaluable.

Paul and Ahlmira, you have demonstrated that Heaven on earth is a family business.

My office staff, Leanne and Janelle, thanks for the hours of ideas and work you both put into this book.

Ken Gire, thanks for spending hours with me talking about the message of this book and coming alongside me as a friend and mentor in helping me learn how to express my heart through the printed word.

Don Milam, thank you for believing in me. The staff at Destiny Image, thank you for your support and help.

To the editor, probably the most vital and least thanked, thank you for helping me fulfill this dream.

I would love to thank my friends, and I am fully aware that I might leave someone out. You all really do know who you are and each of you has been a steady presence in my life. I really appreciate your input, from spiritual impartations to laughs on the phone to down time. Thank you!

Thank you to my friends and family at Bethel (Redding and Atlanta), Global Awakening, and others from coast to coast and around the world. Be blessed!

ENDORSEMENTS

Leif Hetland has somehow managed to capture the heart of the Father with mere words. As I read this book, his words became like arrows, thrusting themselves into my heart. At times I found my soul scrambling for cover, overwhelmed by my own frailness. Like a skilled physician, Leif diagnoses the disease of humanity and prescribes the perfect cure.

Seeing Through Heaven's Eyes is a convicting, convincing novel of love and the dance of passion. Leif summons his audience to leave their seats and waltz with God. But readers BEWARE...you need to be prepared to change BEFORE you read this book! Leif's personal stories will ravage your heart and transform your mind. You will have a hard time putting this book down.

It you are dry, empty, exhausted or bored, Leif's words will kiss you into the next realm. I highly recommend this book to anyone who is hungry for more of Heaven.

KRIS VALLOTTON
Co-Founder of Bethel School of Supernatural Ministry
Author of seven books, including *The Supernatural Ways of Royalty*
Senior Associate Leader of Bethel Church, Redding, California

Leif Hetland's latest book, *Seeing Through Heaven's Eyes*, is a powerful presentation of the love of God for people. It has a strong message of hope for all people, of God's love for all nations.

Leif resets the focus of our cameras through which we see God. His recalibration of the face of God as revealed in Jesus is most helpful. I loved the way Leif leads us on the journey of refocusing how we see reality; the reality of God, the true perspective of ourselves, and the true perspective of others. I especially loved the fourth and last part of the book that dealt with how to see the future. Not through the eyes of defeat where the end time of the world and the Church is painted with dark colors of gloom, doom, death, and defeat, but a picture painted with bright colors of the end as hope filled, a glorious victory for the Kingdom of God. He reminds us that Heaven comes to Earth, paradise lost is paradise regained.

If you want a recalibration of the lens through which you see life, God, yourself, your enemies, and others who are in places of darkness; if you want a better, truer, perspective on life now and life as it can be, as well as the future, this is a great book to help calibrate the lens through which you see life. It will help you learn how to see reality through Heaven's Eyes.

RANDY CLARK

Founder of the Apostolic Network of Global Awakening, Global School of Supernatural Ministry, Multiple Schools of Healing and Impartation, Author of *There Is More; God Can Use Little Ole Me; Lighting Fires; Power, Holiness, and Evangelism*; and many other books; Apostolic Evangelist and Revivalist.

To quote Leif: *This book is about the Father's love, about how He brought the world into existence as a stage upon which that love could be seen, heard, and felt by all.* If you are a believer, you have some understanding that God loves you. However, life experiences and familiarity with that truth can dull our awareness of the reality of that love. With great personal vulnerability, Leif shares his own journey in rediscovering the Father's love and shows us how that perception colors everything in our lives. May Leif's insights shower you with a fresh impartation of Papa's love for you!

JANE HANSEN HOYT
President/CEO
Aglow International

This uplifting book will give you new eyes to see God's purposes in the world. It combines fresh insight into the way God sees us and how we should see others. You will not be able to put this book down!'

R. T. KENDALL
Former Minister
Westminster Chapel, London, England

Leif received an amazing impartation of the Father's love. He provokes me to jealousy. In "Seeing Through Heaven's Eyes", he will impart this love to you and leave you with a passion for joining the "dance" of life that God has set before you.

SID ROTH
Host
"It's Supernatural"

We are born being taught to depend on ourselves – our senses, our reasoning or our emotions. When this doesn't seem to bring the results we seek, we then look to others who have the same limited senses, ability to reason and corrupted emotions.

It is God's plan for us to become exhausted with human impute whether ourselves or others. Leif Hetland has clearly presented God's design for His children to live. Read this book and let God teach you what it means in your life.

ROBERT S. MCGEE
Author of *The Search for Significance*

Leif's book, *Seeing Through Heavens Eyes* is profound! Think about the title. The very moment you shift to seeing from a heavenly perspective - everything changes!

The idea of seeing ourselves, or heavens culture, or each other through heavens eyes, seems like a subject so important and compelling that someone should have written about it long ago. But God hid it from others so the right man could write about it at the right time. Leif is that man. There is no other author who embodies the practice of a heavenly perspective more tangibly or courageously. This book is an important addition to the library of anyone who longs to see, hear and feel heaven on earth.

LANCE WALLNAU
President
The Lance Learning Group

As a follower of Jesus trapped in my humanity I often tell myself "God sees that person or situation totally different than us". The seed of Heavens kingdom can become so buried inside of us from the cares of this world that it becomes difficult to see the real Jesus. I believe this book will help countless believers and non-believers realize God really does love them with an undying Love.

LENNY LEBLANC
International Singer and Song Writer

John the Baptist sent two of his followers to ask Jesus if he really was the Messiah. Jesus said, "Go back to John and tell him what you have seen and heard – *the blind see....*" There are many types of blindness which can prevent a person from seeing what's right in front of them. Of course, our eyes can blind us, but so can our emotions or our lack of faith. Through scripture and the best of stories Leif will help you to see new things about God, his kingdom, and you. Enjoy the book....and see for yourself.

BILL BOHLINE
Lead Pastor
Hosanna! Church

If there were a dictionary in heaven where you could look up "The great commandant," it would say: "See Leif Hetland." I met Leif through a mutual friend, went to one of his conferences, saw him pray for people for hours afterwards, and met with him personally on a number of occasions. I have never met a man who loved God and other people more purely or more passionately. Seeing his heart in person and seeing it expressed in his book, *Seeing Through Heaven's Eyes*, has had a profound impact on my life. Some books you read for information, some you read for inspiration, this one you will read for transformation. My life has been forever changed by it. And so will yours.

KEN GIRE
Author of *Moments with the Savior* and *Windows of the Soul*

Seeing through heaven's eyes" is a wonderful book that leads us back to the simplicity of knowing The Father's heart and knowing who we are in Him. It is when we know His heart of love, compassion and mercy, that we are able to love our neighbor as we love ourselves and bring lasting change to those around us.

Leif Hetland is a passionate lover of Jesus Christ and his passion as an evangelist is an inspiration for all of us. It is a privilege to recommend his book.

HEIDI BAKER, PHD
Founding Director, Iris Ministries

Allow the Holy Spirit to transform your sight as your gaze becomes aligned with Heaven during the pages of this book, transforming every aspect of your life.

CHÉ AHN
Senior Pastor, HROCK Church, Pasadena, California
President, Harvest International Ministry
International Chancellor, Wagner Leadership Institute

Wow! That is not the normal word I would use when reviewing most manuscripts. Sometimes a writer will have good concepts, but are not able to communicate very well. Sometimes authors have poetic language, but no substance. Leif Hetland's work has great content coupled with great communication. I have nothing to offer or suggest. That is also rare for me.

This work is a romanticizing of theology, taking it out of the realm of the classroom and placing it in the world where we live. You have combined all the elements I love in a good book: fresh and creative presentation of ancient truth, leaning on your own personal experiences, bringing in outside sources that accentuate your unveiling of the things Father has shown you and finally incorporating examples from our culture like examples from movies we love (Jerry McGuire and Bucket List). You appeal to the deepest longing of the human soul. Great job!

DON MILAM
Destiny's VP Acquisitions

This book packs a wallop! Leif imparts a life changing message on the power of seeing God, seeing yourself, and your future through the eyes of heaven and the heart of God. You will discover God's desire to unleash Himself into your daily life. This book is a revelatory experience that will propel you into your own spiritual revolution. Leif lives his life in acquaintance with intimacy with God and the supernatural. I've sat up late and laughed with him and observed him in Pakistan in the most dangerous of situations. This man is real! I highly recommend this book as a "must read". It's transforming!

BOB PHILLIPS
Senior Pastor, Encourager Church, Houston, TX

The more you see the more you will see there is to be seen. It is an exciting adventure, a surprise around every corner, never a dull moment, horizons cracking, new horizons looming, every possession an invitation to possess more, every solution gives the key to further solutions. You're on the tiptoe of expectancy, life beckons.
—E. Stanley Jones[1]

CONTENTS

PREFACE

You are holding in your hands a very special book. So special, in fact, that were its truths applied it would be, not like a perfect storm, devastating and disastrous, but like a perfect calm, breaking over a region, business, church, home or person. We are living in a world being torn apart by catastrophes, wars, crimes of every conceivable nature and the very fabric of sense and sensibility is being torn apart.

Leif Hetland refuses to dwell on the apparently hopeless situation of the whole human family on earth and determines to discover the one issue that will set it all straight. He shrugs his shoulders at the obvious and intensely examines the possible. He has the daring to believe that amid all the chaos of earth there is one thing, and only One that holds the key to hope. Not just the hope of survival but the hope of overcoming, of coming to grips with all that grips us in this wild and wicked world.

The author of this book has made hope his passion and love his way of life. Love to him is more than a remarkable emotion to be studied, examined and presented; it is a lifestyle. This lifestyle of love is a commodity forged in the fires of desperation, intense suffering and pain, rejection and betrayal. Leif is a spiritual son of mine and I have been drawn into the adventure of his collision with unconditional love. He is one of the most amazing people I have ever known.

My wife, Friede, has known him longer than I and owes to him her undying passion for Jesus Christ and an amazing anointing to minister in the power of the Spirit of God. While we are both certain that it was God Who led us together, it was Leif who was the human agent who initially introduced us to each other. I would suffer my wife to love no other man like she loves him were it not for the fact that we both love him equally with the strong possibility that mine might be slightly greater.

I have watched him, counseled him, listened to him, preached with him, wept with him and walked with him. I have seen him go to hell and back with my encouragement to take the trip. Ninety-nine men out of a hundred would have collapsed and not survived. Leif seized the tragic day and obediently molded it into a spiritual experience that has made him a true world-changer. I have watched him go through unimaginable pain and hardships and come out the other side victorious, changed and held in the blessed grip of unconditional love.

This volume is the result of all he has gone through and his proper response to God, himself and others. Some folks hide behind what has happened to them and point to unfortunate things that made them the way they are. Leif has taken full responsibility for unfortunate choices on his part, accepted the results with patient obedience, and has given new meaning to loving God, others and himself. He is riveted yet to much pain, a matter we will pray about until resolved. In the meanwhile he continues to walk in human weakness with powerful and consistent resiliency. He has already touched the world including, the Muslim world. In a world that knows next to nothing about love, he has been called the apostle of love.

Seeing Through Heaven's Eyes entails seeing all the things that others see but determines that they are seen through eyes of absolutely unconditional love. This book represents the only hope for this muddled world in an attractive and uncomplicated manner and deserves a wide reading, which I am rather certain, it will receive.

JACK TAYLOR
President Dimensions Ministries
Melbourne, Florida

FOREWORD

One of the greatest privileges in my life is to spend time with leaders in the body of Christ, many of whom have international influence. Over time, relationships are built and partnerships developed, and this amazing mystery called *Life in the Kingdom* unfolds in the only true context for growth: family. When a relationship of substance is built, not only do we have access to the stories of great success and significant impact, but also we have a look into the things that bring a challenge to our faith, and to what causes grief and pain. Such is the case in my friendship with the author of this book, Leif Hetland

It has been a great honor to co-labor with him in training people for living in the pleasure of God. Hearing his heart and watching his life has moved me deeply. I have watched as a man I already admired and had extreme love and respect for went through what many would call *the dark night of the soul*. I watched this highly gifted and favored man return to the one thing that mattered most to him, being a son. For all of us these values can only be proven as authentic when we back up our claims with choices that cost us. And such has been the case in Leif's life. I've watched him back up his value of sonship by joyfully paying a price that many don't even know exists.

I could easily impress you with Leif's life and ministry by sharing just a few of the amazing statistics that surround him. If I were to share with you just a small number of the seemingly unlimited stories of modern day miracles, I could forever endear you to this man of God. If I only wrote about his influence on the *darker* nations of the world, you'd likely make him one of your heroes for a lifetime. But to be consistent with the theme of this book, I want to do my best to present him to you as a son: a really good son, who has become a really good father. He sees differently.

Seeing Through Heaven's Eyes is a book that challenges our perspectives on life and works to reestablish the values that Jesus modeled better than anyone. The changes prescribed on these pages are nothing short of revolutionary, if followed. They are certain to drive a nail into the coffin of religion and set hearts on a course that truly lives in the pleasure of God for a lifetime. This book is refreshingly honest while also being eternally hopeful. This is no small matter, for it determines whether or not our lives are spent for what really matters or for things that will only embarass us in the days to come.

Out of this man's *dark night of the soul* has come forth a sunrise of hope that could impact the lives of believers for generations. It is that good. It is that important. Read it, not for information, although priceless information fills every page. Read it as though it were the ticket to a journey that will impact the rest of your life, right into eternity

BILL JOHNSON
Senior Pastor, Bethel Church, Redding, CA
Author of *When Heaven Invades Earth* and *Dreaming with God*

INTRODUCTION

As they were leaving Jericho, a large crowd followed Him. And two blind men sitting by the road, hearing that Jesus was passing by, cried out, "Lord, have mercy on us, Son of David!" The crowd sternly told them to be quiet, but they cried out all the more, "Lord, Son of David, have mercy on us!" And Jesus stopped and called them, and said, "What do you want Me to do for you?" They said to Him, "Lord, we want our eyes to be opened." Moved with compassion, Jesus touched their eyes; and immediately they regained their sight and followed Him (Matthew 20:29-34 NASB).

The two men in the story were both blind, and both desperate. They knew that this was not simply their *best* chance to regain their sight, it was their *only* chance. If Jesus passed them by, they were destined to spend the rest of their lives on that dry, dusty road, with only the stories of others to give them something to hope for some time in some distant future.

But who knew when?

Who knew when Jesus would be back there?

Who knew if He would *ever* be back there?

So for them, it was now or never. They heard the crowd coming, like the distant roll of thunder before a storm. They smelled the kicked-up dust, felt the change in the air. As the people bustled down the road toward them, they heard the excitement like the sweep of leaves before a sudden wind. "Jesus! He's coming! Make way!"

Words like *miracle worker* and *Messiah* and *Man of God* fell like scraps of bread from a rich man's table into the eager hands of the two beggars. They devoured each morsel. Hungry for more, they reached out toward the crowd, only to have their hands slapped away.

Feeling their chance slipping by, the two called out to this miracle worker whom they could not see, but sensed like a great stillness before a storm.

"Lord, have mercy on us, Son of David!"

The crowd brusquely pushed them aside, telling them to shut up. But the men cried out even more loudly, more persistently.

"Lord, Son of David, have mercy on us!"

And that cry—that marginalized, pushed-aside, desperate cry for mercy—stopped the King of kings in His tracks.

The crowd grew suddenly still and stood on tiptoes, craning their necks, straining their eyes, cupping their ears.

Jesus looked at the haggard men, who were standing now.

Then, in a string of one-syllable words that a child could understand, Jesus asked a simple question: "What do you want Me to do for you?"

The voice was kind and soft and not the least bit hurried or perturbed—just the opposite, in fact. From the sound of His voice, it felt as if all time stood still and was waiting with bated breath. Indeed it was. Angels, no doubt, were part of the procession, standing on the fringe of the crowd; with them, craning their necks; with them, straining their eyes; with them, cupping their ears. For the whole creation had waited on tiptoes for the coming of this promised seed who would one day restore the paradise that had been lost.

Today, at least a portion of that paradise would be restored. Like a cool breeze from Eden, the still pools of their blind eyes would be troubled and healed. As it passed, that breeze would rustle the fallen leaves of that forgotten garden with the fragrantly unfurling scents of the Kingdom of God.

The two blind men couldn't believe it. The Son of David, the Lord of all creation, asking what *He* could do for *them*.

The humility of the moment caused the air around them to tremble.

Then, with the simplicity of a child asking his papa to reach for something out of his grasp, one of them answers:

"Lord, we want our eyes to be opened."

Before Jesus healed them, the text says that His heart went out to them. He saw them, *really* saw them. He saw the furrows between their ribs; saw their spindly legs; saw the gaunt valleys that were their cheeks; saw the sunken holes that held their fixed, unfocused eyes. He smelled them, too, and imagined in a moment all the heartache that life on that road had been for them. He felt for them, deeply, *then* He reached out to them, touching their eyes.

"Immediately they regained their sight," the text says.

"And followed Him," it concludes, almost as an afterthought.

Doubtless they followed Him. For the rest of their joyous, grateful, adventurously expectant lives they followed Him.

How could it be otherwise?

What those two men needed was not instruction but an encounter. They didn't need to go to a conference on miracles; they needed a miracle to come to them. They needed to be touched and healed. But first, they needed to be heard and seen.

They needed eyes of love to behold them—not eyes of judgment, scorn, or ridicule. Eyes of love. The way the eyes of a parent sees their dearly beloved child. The way the eyes of Heaven see us.

Which is what *you* need, isn't it?

And what *I* need.

It is what *all of us* need.

I didn't realize that when I first became a Christian. When I became a Christian, I was baptized with water. After that, a lot in my life changed. A year later, I was baptized in the Spirit, and a lot more changed. But it wasn't until years later when I experienced the "baptism of love" that *everything* changed.

This book chronicles those changes.

It is a book about learning to see through the eyes of Heaven, which is to say, through the eyes of our Father in Heaven. It is not a book about learning to see in the spiritual realm. My friend, Jonathan Welton, does a wonderful job with that in his book, *The School of the Seers: A Practical Guide on How to See in the Unseen Realm.*

Instead of a guide on how to see in *unseen* realms, mine is more of a guide on how to see into *unloved* realms—those places in each of us, for example, where our darkest secrets cower like sightless cave dwellers; those places where the light has not yet reached; those dank, suffocating places where darkness reigns and shame is given not only a place to live, but to thrive.

Can you see that place in the deep recesses of your heart?

Do you shudder at the sight of it? Does it embarrass you whenever you think about all that dwells there? Would it shock your family and friends if they could see those places?

Now, let's look at those same places but with other eyes.

How do you think those places look through Heaven's eyes? How do they look to the Father who loves you? Is He critical of what He sees there? Or is He filled with compassion? Do you think He wants to seal off the entrance to that dark cave...or to flood it with the light of His presence? Does He want to bring judgment to the part of you that has squandered its inheritance...or does He want to run to that prodigal part, shower it with kisses, bring it home, and celebrate its return?

How you see yourself—and your secrets—is directly related to how you see God.

If you see God as judgmental, you will likely see yourself harshly and treat yourself harshly. If you see God as loving, you will likely see yourself tenderly and treat yourself tenderly.

What we need to change is the way we see.

It would be nice if that change would be as easy as an eye exam and a prescription for corrective lenses. Or even Lasik surgery, which is a relatively simple procedure with little pain or discomfort. But what we are talking about is not a change of vision so much as it is a change of heart.

Which is the work of the Spirit.

Before the Spirit changed my heart, I used to have some of the same short-sightedness, some of the same astigmatisms, and some of the same blindness as the religious leaders that Jesus spoke against. Even though I had attended Bible college and seminary, and even though I was pastoring a church, I suffered from a kind of macular-degenerative disease that kept me from seeing myself and those around me through the loving eyes of my Heavenly Father.

The reason I couldn't see myself or others correctly was because I couldn't see Him correctly.

After that encounter with the Holy Spirit, I no longer looked at God as an angry, austere authority figure. I saw Him as a kind, tenderhearted God of love. He was my Papa, and I was His dearly beloved son. I no longer saw myself as a slave, working for wages, but rather as a son, living off his inheritance. I saw others differently, too. I no longer saw them through the harsh glare of judgment but through the soft gaze of love. Even the future looked different. Through Heaven's eyes there was nothing to fear about the end times; instead, I found so much to love, which was startling and, at the same time, exhilarating.

Since that experience, I began seeing everything through different eyes. So drastic were the changes in clarity, color, and perspective in the spiritual realm that it was as if I had been like one of those blind men, sitting on the side of the road while the world of the sighted was passing me by.

Like Dorothy in *The Wizard of Oz,* I was whisked up in a whirlwind of an experience, and when I was plopped down, I knew I wasn't in Kansas anymore. The eyes of my heart were enlightened. I went from seeing in sepia tones to stunning technicolors. I saw God differently, myself differently, other people differently, even the future differently.

This book will take you on a miraculous journey through dangers in dark, lifeless countries to delights in bright, edenic parts of the world where the Kingdom of God has come near.

I hardly have words to describe the adventure I have been on the past several years. The closest I can come to describing them is Eugene Peterson's translation of Romans 8:15-17a in The Message:

This resurrection life you received from God is not a timid, grave-tending life. It's adventurously expectant, greeting God with a childlike "What's next, Papa?" God's Spirit touches our spirits and confirms who we really are. We know who He is, and we know who we are: Father and children. And we know we are going to get what's coming to us—an unbelievable inheritance!

You are in for an adventure!

Be expectant, greeting God with a childlike, "What's next, Papa?"

Papa is going to put you on His big, broad shoulders and show you some amazing things!

He's going to show you who *He* is. He's going to show you who *you* are. And He's going to show you the happily-ever-after ending He has in store for all His children.

But before we get started, let me pray for you.

AUTHOR'S PRAYER

Papa God,

I am just a boy, but I am Your boy, which makes all the difference in the world and how I view it.

For without You, I can do nothing.

But with You, I can do all things.

My hands are so small, Papa, but when I put them in Your big hands, there is nothing I can't do.

My stature is so short, but when You boost me up and put me on Your shoulders, there is nothing I can't see.

My legs are so weak, but when You let me stand on Your feet, there is no place I can't go.

My words are so few and so meager, like the boy with the few slender fish and the coarsely ground loaves.

What are they when the hunger in the soul is so great?

Take them in Your hands—Your big, strong hands—and multiply them.

Bless them in the life of the person who is about to read this book.

May the eyes of her heart—or his—be enlightened to see how good You are and how very valuable she is…or how very valuable he is.

I pray that the Holy Spirit would plunge the reader into a baptism of love.

May all who immerse themselves in these words come up from the water, dripping in Your Spirit, drenched in Your love.

Help them to glimpse the delight in Your eyes when they look up, to see how very proud You are to have them as Your children.

Let them see Your glowing face and Your glistening eyes.

As they see themselves as You see them, help them to see others as You see them.

Help them to see Your compassion going out to the pimp as well as to the prostitute.

Help them see Your love reaching out to the pharisaical brother, working away in his father's fields, as well as to the prodigal one, wasting away in the distant country.

Help them see Your mercy extended to Ishmael as well as to Isaac, and Your hand cupped around the dimly burning wick of the elderly in hospice care as well as the preemie in intensive care.

Help the reader to look at the future not anxiously but expectantly, not as the destruction of all things but as the redemption of all things.

In the name of Your dearly beloved Son, my brother, my Savior, my King. Amen.

PART 1

SEEING GOD THE WAY JESUS SEES HIM

The goal of creation is to "glorify God" (see Ps. 86:9; John 12:28; 17:1). God's glory is the radiant display of the divine nature. As God's life is poured into individuals and flows through individuals to other people, we individually and collectively "image" God....

This is the goal of everything. It is the reason why anything other than God even exists. As God is the one being who exists in and of Himself, so God's love is the one reality that is an end in and of itself. We might say that the goal of every individual, and of humanity in general, is to dance the eternal dance of the Trinity, to participate in and glorify this unsurpassably loving fellowship.

We do this by receiving and reflecting the unsurpassable love that God is.

A more beautiful vision of creation is not imaginable. —Gregory A. Boyd[1]

CHAPTER 1

SEEING GOD IN HIS GLORY

The heavens declare the glory of God; and the firmament shows His handiwork. Day unto day utters speech, and night unto night reveals knowledge (Psalm 19:1-2).

Since the dawn of time, the universe has been trying to make contact with us. The irony is that, while we have spent millions on projects like SETI (Search for Extraterrestrial Intelligence), we haven't gotten the message.

Day after day, night after night, David says, the heavens have been shouting it; the earth has been showing it.

"Look at this! See that! Here it is! And there! Look, it's over there, too!"

The glory of God is everywhere.

And all creation has been trying to get us to see it.

David was overwhelmed with it. Read through the Psalms. See him point to things in the night sky as if he were a wide-eyed boy seeing it for the first time (see Ps. 8). Hear the excitement in his voice as he compares the sunrise to a bridegroom coming out of his tent the morning after his wedding night, beaming with joy and bursting with vigor (see Ps. 19). Feel the trembling awe as he describes God's intricate stitch-work in knitting together nerves and muscles, arteries and capillaries, ligaments and tendons of the unborn (see Ps. 139).

The creation was meant to overwhelm us, not with its beauty, complexity, or majesty, but with the One who is responsible for its beauty, its complexity, its majesty.

Most of the time, though, we are overwhelmed with other, lesser things.

Lesser galaxies. Lesser glories. Lesser gods.

Allow me to get personal for a moment and ask a question.

What overwhelms you?

Today. Now. As you are reading this. Are you overwhelmed about life? About the life of someone you love? About your own life?

How are you feeling about the explosion of technology? Do you ever wish you could just throw away your cell phone, disconnect your Internet connection, and cancel your email account? Is everything changing so fast that you fear the world is passing you by?

Are you overwhelmed about the staggering weight of credit card debt you are carrying? Is it taking its toll on you, on your marriage? Are you worried about your physical health? How about your mental health?

Are you depressed? Are you afraid to admit you're depressed? Afraid what others will think, how they'll react?

Are you kicking yourself for not saving more for retirement? Do you feel overwhelmed with the very real possibility that you'll have to work until you die?

Are you worried that your brain is starting to slow down? Are you forgetting simple things, like the spelling of familiar words, conversations, basic math? Are you worried that people around you are beginning to notice?

Are you overwhelmed by your workload, wondering how much longer you can take the stress? Is your body beginning to tire more quickly, more easily? Do you find yourself panting after taking a flight of stairs instead of the elevator?

How's your attitude? Are you anxious? Afraid? Angry? Are the muscles in your neck constantly tense with knots in them? Are you short with others? Are you crabby when you get home?

How are you sleeping? Do you need something to help you sleep? Do you grind your teeth at night? How do you feel when you wake up? Do you dread the day ahead of you? What thoughts go through your mind when you stare at the mirror in the morning and you hardly recognize the person staring back?

Are you taking more aspirin? More antacids? Are you drinking to relax? And is it taking more drinks to relax you? Are you becoming more dependent on prescription drugs?

How's your blood pressure?

Is your marriage falling apart? Is one of your kids breaking your heart? Is your job draining the life out of you?

How do you think the Father looks at you when He sees you overwhelmed with such things? Do you picture Him with a disappointed look on His face? Is He shaking His head and saying to Himself, *"Her again. I should have known. When is she ever going to get it together?"*

Or do you picture a disgusted look? *"That does it. That's the last straw. I'm not bailing him out this time. Let him suffer the consequences and see if that doesn't straighten him out."*

Weighed down. Stressed out. Crushed. Brokenhearted. Overwhelmed.

Is that you?

If so, what do you think God is going to do with you?

The Scriptures say He draws near to the brokenhearted, to the crushed of spirit (see Ps. 34:18). And why? Does He draw near to get a closer look at the mess we've made of our lives? Does He draw near to give us a lecture? A rap across the knuckles? A good beating, or at least a berating?

No. Certainly He doesn't. Then why *does* He draw near?

To *bind up* our wounds (see Ps. 147:3). To clean them, to put salve on them, and to bandage them. He comes to help.

I suspect He does the same with the overwhelmed.

"Come to Me, all you who labor and are heavy laden," Jesus said, "and I will give you…" What? …A piece of My mind? …What you've got coming? …A lesson you'll never forget?

No. He says, "I will give you rest" (see Matt. 11:28). And as He says it, you can almost see the kindness in His eyes, can't you? Almost hear the tenderness in His voice.

How did Jesus respond to the two disciples who were overwhelmed with grief, so brokenhearted as they walked away from everything on that road to Emmaus?

He drew near.

Why?

To help them get their bearings so they could find their way home (see Luke 24:32-33).

Why did Jesus come to people who were overwhelmed? Why did He come to the Widow of Nain who had lost her only son? (See Luke 7:11-16.) Why did He come to the synagogue official whose daughter had died? (See Mark 5:21-43.) Why did He come to the father who was overwhelmed with the care of his epileptic son? (See Matt. 17:14-18.) Why did He come to the woman overwhelmed with seven demons tormenting her? (See Mark 16:9-10.)

Why does He come to any of us who are overwhelmed with the burdens of life?

He comes to heal, to restore, to deliver, to resurrect, to ease our burdens, and to give us rest.

If you are overwhelmed, I'm not here to add to the burdens you are carrying by loading you up with guilt. Being overwhelmed is nothing to feel guilty about. It is part of the geography of the life of faith, like the wilderness. We all end up overwhelmed at some time or another. Moses ended up there, on more than one occasion. Elijah. Jeremiah, frequently. And Paul, so much so that he despaired of life—another way of saying he was suicidal. Even Jesus got overwhelmed, in Gethsemane (see Matt. 26:36-39).

So how do we end up there, you and I?

And how do we get out of there?

To answer those questions, we're going to take a look at a man who found himself overwhelmed a number of times throughout his life—David. In Psalm 57, David has fled from Saul, and he is in hiding out in a cave. He is a long way from the palace, surrounded by enemies, outnumbered, and overwhelmed:

My soul is among lions; I lie among the sons of men who are set on fire, whose teeth are spears and arrows, and their tongue a sharp sword (Psalm 57:4).

Another time, another crisis, and he is overwhelmed again:

Save me, O God! For the waters have come up to my neck. I sink in deep mire, where there is no standing; I have come into deep waters, where the floods overflow me. I am weary with my crying; my throat is dry; my eyes fail while I wait for my God (Psalms 69:1-3).

Here it seems that David is about to give up completely:

For the enemy has persecuted my soul; he has crushed my life to the ground; he has made me dwell in darkness, like those who have long been dead. Therefore my spirit is overwhelmed within me; my heart within me is distressed (Psalm 143:3-4).

So how did David get over being overwhelmed with his circumstances?

He got overwhelmed with God: *"Be exalted, O God, above the heavens; let Your glory be above all the earth"* (Ps. 57:5).

Here he takes his eyes off his circumstances and onto the character of God:

Hear me, O LORD, for Your lovingkindness is good; turn to me according to the multitude of Your tender mercies. And do not hide Your face from Your servant, for I am in trouble; hear me speedily (Psalm 69:16-17).

Finally, he goes back in his memory, remembering the greatness of God: *"I remember the days of old; I meditate on all Your works; I muse on the work of Your hands"* (Ps. 143:5).

In each case, David regained his bearings. How? By looking up. By finding what had always been his North Star and focusing on it to find his way back to a place of faith. Whether he was in a disorienting wilderness, some confining cave, or surrounded by an impossible set of circumstances, David was always looking up, always getting overwhelmed by God—overwhelmed by His goodness, His greatness, His glory.

It is a sobering truth, but a truth nonetheless—either we will be overwhelmed by God...or we will be overwhelmed by everything else.

In view of that, here are some options to consider. Are you currently:

Overwhelmed by the glory of God...or overwhelmed by your finances?

Overwhelmed by the glory of God...or overwhelmed by your family?

Overwhelmed by the glory of God…or overwhelmed by the future?

Your choice—overwhelmed by awe…or by anxiety?

A question to consider before making your choice: Do you want to spend the rest of your life worrying or worshiping?

Awe is a prerequisite to worship. If we are not being filled with awe on a regular basis, we will not be overflowing with worship on a regular basis, at least not the way David worshipped—passionately.

I know that some of you are thinking you've got a handle on life and are doing fine managing your own. Here's another thing you need to hear. We are all a heartbeat away from disaster…a heartache away from divorce…a heart attack away from death.

A drunk driver, an affair, a piece of plaque breaking lose and clogging an artery, and life is never the same. It can happen to any of us at any time. We are all only a diagnosis away from devastation—cancer, Alzheimer's, M.S.

Maybe none of those things overwhelm you. Maybe it's something deeper, something no one sees or suspects. Maybe you are overwhelmed with guilt from a secret sin…overwhelmed with defeat from a destructive addiction…overwhelmed with shame from a painful past.

What do you do then?

Oscar Wilde, a writer who struggled a lot with life, once said, "We are all in the gutter, but some of us are looking up at the stars."[1]

David looked up when he found himself in his own gutter after stealing another man's wife, having the man killed to legalize the theft and legitimize the marriage, and then covering it all up as if nothing happened. Finally overwhelmed by guilt, with his body wasting away, David looked up and saw three shining stars that helped him find his way home—the graciousness of God, the lovingkindness of God, and the compassion of God (see Ps. 51:1 NASB).

Let's follow David's lead and look up at the stars. We'll see if we can get overwhelmed, too.

On a clear night in the country, with no city lights to dim the view or pollution to blur it, the human eye can see between two and three thousand stars. Most appear the size of a grain of sand. For purposes of comparison, let's use that as a standard of measure. The grain of sand closest to us is our own sun, which is 93 million miles away. The second closest grain is Proxima Centauri, part of the Alpha Centauri system. It is 4.35 light years away. That doesn't sound *too* far away—until you do the math. A light year is a measurement of time that it takes light to travel in one year. Since light travels at 186,000 miles per second, or 670 million miles per hour, a beam of light can travel to the sun in just 8 minutes. But to reach the next closest star, Proxima Centauri, it takes over four years.

Now imagine this. Around the grain of sand that is our sun is a cluster of other stars. That is the Milky Way. As late as the 1920s, it was thought that the Milky Way was the entire universe. Then in 1923, Edwin Hubble photographed the Andromeda galaxy, 2.5 light years away. Now, the Hubble Space Telescope, launched in 1990 and orbiting 375 miles above the Earth, has been able to photograph images billions of miles away.

With Hubble's discoveries and the telescope named after him, all calculations had to be revised. The Milky Way, the galaxy that looks like a wide river of stardust meandering through the night sky, is actually a spiral-shaped galaxy that is about a hundred thousand light years across and ten thousand light years wide. How many stars are in that vast expanse of space? Between two and four hundred billion. To stay with our measure of a grain of sand representing a star, it would take a really large dump truck to hold them all.

As for the universe itself, if a train of railroad cars were filled with sand that represented all the stars in the known universe, and if the railroad cars passed by you at the rate of one per second, 24 hours a day, 7 days a week, it would take three years for all the sand-filled cars to pass by.[2]

All those stars, those galaxies, those supernovas, those nebulae, those cosmic wonders strewn throughout the universe like so many grains of sand—*God did that!* What is greater—He did it with a *word* (see Heb. 11:3)! A word that is sharper than a two-edged sword, we are told, even to the dividing of soul and spirit, joints and marrow (see Heb. 4:12). A word so strong it can spin a galaxy, so sharp it can splice a gene.

Hearing David's boyish enthusiasm about the wonder he experienced watching the night skies reminds me of the wonder I experienced as a boy growing up on the shores of the North Sea.

Ever since I can remember I have had a longing for belonging. I didn't find it in church, so I went looking for it in other places. One of the places that drew me was the sea. Our home was in Haugesund on the southwest coast of Norway. In back of our house were the mountains; in front was the sea—a great, gray expanse of water that stretched across the far reaches of my imagination. Every day from the time I was nine until I was almost grown, the sea and its shores were my playground. My dreams, stories, and adventures were all played out against that backdrop.

Staring out over that sea, a lighthouse stood as if a dutiful sailor in dress-whites, standing at attention, watching out for boats in distress. At night, the vigilant sentry swept its beam over the sea, however fierce the wind, however frothy the waves. For all the years I played along those shores, its presence comforted me, as if it were watching out for me as well.

In winter, I cut holes in the ice to jump in the freezing water and show off to my friends. In warmer weather, I played along its rocky shores, exploring the smaller universes of tide pools, teeming with almost otherworldly life forms. On the shoreline I played in tunnels that had been burrowed by Polish prisoners of war whom the Germans had used as forced labor. I found helmets and spent shells, oblivious to the horrors of war or to the cruelties against its prisoners. I thought only of play—of cowboys and Indians, of hunting for treasures, of basking in the summer sun as the sea filled the air with the scent of its mysteries that mingled beneath the surface.

My dad and grandfather often took me fishing in the dark, choppy waters of that sea. When the weather was violent, though, I stayed indoors, looking through binoculars as huge boats were tossed by its waves like plastic toys in kiddie pools. The view from the picture window in my living room was an ever-changing seascape, with jutting rocks and crashing waves, soft-pastel sunrises and bold-brushed sunsets, torrential rains, and blinding snowstorms.

The sea nourished me in ways it's hard to describe. I respected it but didn't fear it. It was this old, gray benefactor who gave so much, asking nothing in return. The gifts the sea gave me were companionship, solitude, a place where my imagination could roam, intriguing rocks and exotic shells, wraith-like limbs of driftwood, carcasses of sea creatures washed up on its shores, and horizons that called to me with promises of daring adventures and dazzling treasures.

The fjord that carried the Vikings to other lands was the same fjord that carried my grandpa and father to sea in their youth. I watched while, on calm days, cruise ships and even the King's ship traveled this sea. It treated them all the same, this great equalizer—yet another thing I learned from this sage teacher, yet another gift from the sea.

In summer, we had long hours of sunshine. In winter, the days were short, with darkness coming around four in the afternoon. And when I woke up in the morning, it was *still* dark. But the darkness had its own gifts to give. On some nights, it looked as if some beneficent monarch had reached into his treasure chest and cast his wealth across an endless expanse of black velvet—a glittering array of diamonds, sapphires, and pearls.

It was absolutely mesmerizing. Because of where we lived, we didn't have bright city lights dimming the view, and we didn't have pollution obscuring the view. On a cloudless, moonless night, you could see forever. The Milky Way seemed a highway through the heavens, paved with flecks of stars.

Surrounded as I was by such glories, day and night, it was hard *not* to believe in God. It was hard not to believe wonderful things about Him. He was *powerful,* that was easy to see, *all*-powerful. Who could match Him? He was *wonderful*—full of wonders, literally. And He was *beautiful.* How could one responsible for such beauty *not* be? He was *generous,* too. Even as a young boy I realized *that.* So many extravagant gifts, given so freely.

Paul says as much in Romans:

The basic reality of God is plain enough. Open your eyes and there it is! By taking a long and thoughtful look at what God has created, people have always been able to see...[His] eternal power... and the mystery of His divine being (Romans 1:19-20 MSG).

One of the great mysteries of the universe is what makes up the core of galaxies, including our own Milky Way. Astronomers discovered that a swirling mystery, known as a black hole, sits right in the middle of it, sucking stars into its vortex like a cosmic vacuum cleaner. A black hole is a mass so dense that its gravitational pull won't even allow light to escape from it. Recently astronomers learned that this black hole is 27,000 light years from Earth with a mass that is four million times bigger than our sun. The closer a star gets to that mysterious center of our galaxy, the more it is in danger of being drawn to its death.

For me, this raises the question about the mystery of *God's* being.

What is *that* core like, and how dangerous is it if you get too close? I learned, even as a little boy, that God is a lot of things. He is just, for example. But justice is not the core of His being. He is holy, too, but holiness is not the core of who He is. He is also almighty, but power is not the essence of who He is.

Then what is?

We are told by the disciple who was closest to Jesus that the core of God's being is love (see 1 John 4:8b).

If that is true, then love motivates everything He does, including the creation. Peter Kreeft has written as much in his book, *Heaven, the Heart's Deepest Longing:*

> The whole world is a love letter. The haunting of romantic love is the clue to the central theme of the story; it tells us the kind of story we are in. All artistry reflects the artist; and if God is love, then his world is the eternal love made visible in time.[3]

I take comfort that the center of God's being is not a black hole but a beautiful heart. His heart doesn't take life but gives life; His heart brims with love, spinning it out from itself, not sucking it into itself. I felt something of that love spill onto me like ocean spray whenever I was out in nature, especially when I was near the sea or under the stars.

Eventually, though, I grew up, leaving Norway, our home, and that great playground by the sea. I became an adult, shedding my childlike wonder like so many outgrown clothes. I went off to college, then to seminary, where most of my time was spent reading densely written books of theology in libraries, not the elaborately illuminated manuscripts of God in nature.

I thought of the sea—and of the sky above it—less and less. I stopped looking up, and I stopped being overwhelmed with the glory of God. I lost my sense of awe, and I forgot how to worship, *really* worship. After graduating with a degree in theology, I went to work in a church. I fell in love, got married, had children. Years passed. I returned to Norway with my son when *he* graduated. The shores of the North Sea had been his playground whenever we went to visit Far Mor and Far Far

(Grandma and Grandpa) when *he* was a child. Together we walked those same shores, stared out across that same sea, looked up at that same sky. He was swept up in the wonder of it all, the beauty and grandeur of it all. He was overwhelmed. Through him, I saw it all again through renewed eyes. He went out, rain or shine, and drank it all in. It was his dreaming place, his confidant, his partner in adventure. Watching him was like watching myself as a young boy. He showed me how fresh and amazing it all was. I had forgotten that.

Seeing him overwhelmed by the same sea, the same shore, and the same sky that had overwhelmed me, I realized that he shares not only my DNA but also the dreamy side of who I am. I look at him sometimes, and I am filled with awe, for he too is a universe that displays the glory of God—a mysterious, miraculous, majestic universe. Thinking about that brings me back to David and the awe he expressed in Psalm 139:

> *O LORD, You have searched me and known me. You know my sitting down and my rising up; You understand my thought afar off. You comprehend my path and my lying down, and are acquainted with all my ways. For there is not a word on my tongue, but behold, O LORD, You know it altogether. You have hedged me behind and before, and laid Your hand upon me. Such knowledge is too wonderful for me; it is high, I cannot attain it. Where can I go from Your Spirit? Or where can I flee from Your presence? If I ascend into heaven, You are there; if I make my bed in hell, behold, You are there. If I take the wings of the morning, and dwell in the uttermost parts of the sea, even there Your hand shall lead me, and Your right hand shall hold me. If I say, "Surely the darkness shall fall on me," even the night shall be light about me; indeed, the darkness shall not hide from You, but the night shines as the day; the darkness and the light are both alike to You. For You formed my inward parts; You covered me in my mother's womb. I will praise You, for I am fearfully and wonderfully made; marvelous are Your works, and that my soul knows very well. My frame was not hidden from You, when I was made in secret, and skillfully wrought*

in the lowest parts of the earth. Your eyes saw my substance, being yet unformed. And in Your book they all were written, the days fashioned for me, when as yet there were none of them. How precious also are Your thoughts to me, O God! How great is the sum of them! If I should count them, they would be more in number than the sand; when I awake, I am still with You (Psalm 139:1-18).

That most worshipful psalm was written by a person in awe. Earlier we saw David overwhelmed by the glory of God in the universe. Now we see him overwhelmed by that same glory in the uterus.

So what does all that mean to you and to me in the overwhelming realities of life in the 21st century?

Precisely this: The universe exists to give us life and to nurture that life. It is designed to provide for us, to protect us, and to awe us. But it is also here to teach us. One of the things it teaches us is how to see through Heaven's eyes. David was a good student in that classroom, perhaps the best—and he has shown us how to see God in the macro *and* in the micro. In doing so, he has shown that there is nowhere we can flee to where the glory, the greatness, and the goodness of God is not present. Heaven teaches us to see the glory of God on a cosmic level and on a cellular level *so that* we can learn to see it on a circumstantial level—specifically, in *your* circumstances and in *mine*. When we see our circumstances through Heaven's eyes, they will never overwhelm us.

There is no problem in our life so large that it is beyond God's control.

There is no detail in our life so small that it is beyond God's concern.

THE READER'S PRAYER

I am overwhelmed by You, God. How eloquently the night sky speaks of Your glory. How grandly the sun-lit earth showcases

Your art. I am overwhelmed that such a God would want me as His child!

How could this be?

Overwhelm me, I pray, with breathtaking awareness that the ruler of the universe is my Dad.

The prophet, Isaiah, asks:

Who has measured the waters in the hollow of His hand, and marked off the heavens by the span, and calculated the dust of the earth by the measure, and weighed the mountains in a balance and the hills in a pair of scales? (Isaiah 40:12 AMP)

And I answer, "That's my Dad!"

Again the prophet speaks:

He it is who reduces rulers to nothing, who makes the judges of the earth meaningless. Scarcely have they been planted, scarcely have they been sown, scarcely has their stock taken root in the earth, but He merely blows on them, and they wither, and the storm carries them away like stubble (Isaiah 40:23-24 AMP).

Again, I affirm, "That's my Dad!"

And finally Isaiah says:

Lift up your eyes on high and see who has created these stars, the One who leads forth their host by number (Isaiah 40:26).

And I say, "That's my Dad!"

Thank You, Dad, that there is no problem in my life so large that it is beyond Your control and no detail in my life so small that is beyond Your concern.

More, God! Show me more! Overwhelm me, again and again and again. Teach me to see my circumstances through Heaven's eyes.

CHAPTER 2

SEEING THE CULTURE OF HEAVEN

*In the beginning God created the heavens and the earth. The
earth was without form, and void; and darkness was on the face
of the deep. And the Spirit of God was hovering over the face of
the waters. Then God said, "Let there be light"; and there was
light* (Genesis 1:1-3).

*In the beginning was the Word, and the Word was with God,
and the Word was God. He was in the beginning with God. All
things were made through Him, and without Him nothing was
made that was made* (John 1:1-3).

*Then God said, "Let **Us** make man in **Our** image, according to
Our likeness"* (Genesis 1:26a).

Earlier this year, before I started writing this book, the Holy Spirit
revealed to me something about the culture of Heaven. He whispered to me, "The rhythm of Heaven is in the waltz."

A blasphemous thought...or a biblical one?

At first I wasn't sure. Then Jesus' words in the parable of the prodigal
son came to mind. The parable opened a window of Heaven to show us
something of what the culture there is like. It is not a dull, boring place
with dull, boring people. It is not a stern, judgmental place with stern,

judgmental people. It was a festive place, full of joy, *"music and dancing"* (Luke 15:25). Even the angels joined in (see Luke 15:10)—and that was if just *one* sinner repented. Imagine the celebration when a bunch of them come home. You would need a grand ballroom to hold the party!

Jesus didn't think it odd to describe the culture of Heaven in terms of a dance. Neither did C.S. Lewis. In his book, *Letters to Malcolm: Chiefly on Prayer,* he wrote this about the unfettered joys of Heaven:

> Dance and game are frivolous, unimportant, down here: for "down here" is not their natural place. Here, they are a moment's rest from the life we were placed here to live. But in this world everything is upside down. That which, if it could be prolonged here, would be a truancy, is likest that which in a better country is the End of ends. Joy is the serious business of Heaven.[1]

"Joy is the serious business of Heaven." And what better way to express joy than by dancing? The idea captivated me. I wasn't a dancer, let alone a waltzer. So I began researching the waltz and listening to waltzes to try to understand what He meant.

The term *waltz,* I learned, is from the German word *walzen,* meaning "to roll, turn, or to glide."[2] Originally a lively, joyful, country dance of the peasants in outlying areas of Vienna and in alpine regions of Austria, it is a simple dance, easily learned. It is characterized by two partners intertwining their arms at shoulder level, often touching cheek to cheek, and moving as one in 3/4 time with strong accent on the first beat and a basic pattern of step, step, close.

After a lot of thought, study, and prayer, I finally understood what the Holy Spirit revealed to me. The analogy that most accurately represents the culture of Heaven is the image of the waltz. There is *love* in the waltz—partners delighting not only in the dance but in each other's company, holding each other, gazing into each other's eyes, whispering into each other's ears. There is *joy* in the waltz—a lively, breathless, exhilarating sense of being swept away. And finally, there is *unity* in the waltz—two partners moving as one, in step not only with the music but with each other.

As I thought about the image of the waltz, it reminded me of the lively, joyful way the Father, the Son, and the Holy Spirit intertwined themselves, moving as one to create the universe.

Even the creation account has a rhythm in the way it was written. "And God said…and there was…and it was good…and there was morning and there was evening."

Feel the graceful movement of the words? They're almost dancing!

In the first verse of Genesis, God the Father is introduced as the one initiating the grand, sweeping movements of creation. In the second verse, God the Holy Spirit is introduced as the one moving over the watery darkness that covered the earth. Although God the Son is not mentioned in the creation account in Genesis, John tells us in the first few verses of his Gospel that He was there, playing an equally vital role alongside the Father and the Holy Spirit (see John 1:1-5). In the beginning, when God spoke, the Spirit and the Son responded by moving in step with His every word, going forward together in great, sweeping movements across the universe (see also Col. 1:16-17).

But why did they create such an extravagant and expansive place that included countless luminaries of breathtaking beauty, light years of distance between each one? The Trinity, dancing in love, joy, and unity, created the universe as their grand ballroom, with galaxies serving as chandeliers and great expanses between the stars for room to kick up their heels.

Love. Joy. Unity. Wherever the Triune God goes, this trinity of virtues accompanies Him. If you ever wonder if God is moving in a person's life or in a congregation's life, look to see how much love is there, how much joy, how much unity. A loveless church is not a church in which

God is moving, let alone dancing—neither is a joyless, or a divided church.

God the Father, God the Son, God the Holy Spirit. So great was their love *for* each other, so great was their joy *in* each other, so great was their unity *with* each other that it was too bountiful to contain, too wonderful to keep to themselves. And so the three of them counseled together as to how they could expand the dance: *"Then God said, 'Let Us make man in **Our** image, according to **Our** likeness'"* (Gen. 1:26).

"Let Us make a partnership that looks like Us," He said, "loves like Us, dances like Us. Let Us extend Our family. Let Us expand the culture of Heaven in an ever-widening circle that will begin with two people and fill the earth with the love, the joy, and the unity We have for each other." Genesis 5 chronicles the beginnings of that circle:

> *This is the book of the genealogy of Adam. In the day that God created man, He made him in the likeness of God. He created them male and female, and blessed them and called them Mankind in the day they were created. And Adam lived one hundred and thirty years, and begot a son in his own likeness, after his image, and named him Seth* (Genesis 5:1-5).

The first family broke the embrace, wanting to do their *own* dance to their *own* music. They stumbled and fell, bringing discord into the world, and it seemed the dance had come to a tragic end. But God still loved them, sought them out, and promised them that blessing would one day overcome the curse, that the music would not die, that the dance would go on. Generation after generation, the dance continued, however awkward the turns, however halting the steps, however embarrassing the stumbles, however painful the falls. The family of God continued to expand. Generation after generation, the seed of hope was passed—to Seth and his family, to Noah and his family, to Abraham and his family, to David and his family. Until at last, the Word of God became flesh to teach a world that had lost its music how to dance again. He started with a group of disciples who became His family, then expanded the circle to include the larger family of the Church.

Before Jesus began His ministry, He was baptized in the Jordan by John the Baptist, a scene in which the dance between the Father, the Son, and the Holy Spirit waltzes through the veil of Heaven; there, in a rare moment, their interaction with each other can be seen and heard here on earth:

> *The moment Jesus came up out of the baptismal waters, the skies opened up and He saw God's Spirit—it looked like a dove—descending and landing on Him. And along with the Spirit, a voice: "This is My Son, chosen and marked by My love, delight of My life"* (Matthew 3:16-17).

In the first verse of the next chapter, Matthew says that the Spirit "led" Jesus into the wilderness to be tested. The wilderness was part of the dance floor, and testing was part of the dance. The Spirit led; the Son followed—both in step with the choreography of the Father.

Later in His ministry, Jesus went to Jerusalem and healed a lame man at the Pool of Bethesda. When questioned by His critics as to why He was healing on the Sabbath, Jesus told them:

> *"My Father is working straight through, even on the Sabbath. So am I." That really set them off. The Jews were now not only out to expose Him; they were out to kill Him. Not only was He breaking the Sabbath, but He was calling God His own Father, putting Himself on a level with God. So Jesus explained Himself at length. "I'm telling you this straight. The Son can't independently do a thing, only what He sees the Father doing. What the Father does, the Son does. The Father loves the Son and includes Him in everything He is doing"* (John 5:17-20a MSG).

Jesus told them, essentially, that He was simply following His Father's lead, just like in dancing. The Father was doing a small dance at the Pool of Bethesda, hoping those gathered there would join in the celebration, but they didn't.

In another place, Jesus scolded His critics for not joining in the joy of what the Father was doing through Him: *"We played the flute for you,"* Jesus said, and the great indictment of them was *"and you did not dance"* (Luke 7:32). The old shaker song, written by Sydney Carter, takes the image Jesus used and extends it into a song.

> I danced for the scribe
> And the Pharisee,
> But they would not dance
> And they wouldn't follow me.
>
> I danced for the fishermen—
> For James and John—
> They came with me
> And the dance went on.
>
> Dance, then, wherever you may be,
> I am the Lord of the Dance, said he,
> And I'll lead you all, wherever you may be,
> And I'll lead you all in the Dance, said he.[3]

Looking at the downtrodden crowd, Jesus felt compassion on them and said,

> *Are you tired? Worn out? Burned out on religion? Come to Me. Get away with Me, and you'll recover your life. I'll show you how to take a real rest. Walk with Me and work with Me—watch how I do it. Learn the unforced rhythm of grace. I won't lay anything heavy or ill-fitting on you. Keep company with Me, and you'll learn to live freely and lightly* (Matthew 11:28-30 MSG).

You see the three members of the Trinity mentioned in the upper room at the last supper (see John 13–17), where Jesus prays that the love, joy, and unity in Heaven would be replicated in them on earth. That circle of love, joy, and unity expanded from the disciples into the early Church. As the family of God continued to grow, so did the dance.

As I told you before, since I was a child, I had a longing for belonging. I never found that belonging at church. I never found it at school, whether it was secondary school, college, or seminary. It wasn't until I got married and had children that I felt I finally belonged.

It was a family that made me feel that way.

It was the culture of Heaven coming down and replicating itself in the earthly culture of Leif and Jennifer Hetland. Out of the love, the joy, and the oneness we shared as husband and wife, came four children: the oldest, a boy; the other three, girls. Each one we longed for; each one we love; each one we take great joy in. Together we are one—a family.

We step on each other's toes sometimes. And sometimes we push each other away. Other times we bump into each other. At times we leave the dance floor altogether, needing to get air, needing our own space, needing to be alone for a while. But we always come back. It's the love that brings us back, and the joy—and because we are family. Six very diverse people, one very delightful family.

Fifteen years ago my family and I were members of a conservative Baptist church in the South. I was the missions pastor. Needless to say, we didn't dance. After one of the services, my wife approached me with a shocking request: "I would love it if you and I could dance together."

She took me completely off guard. I paused a second, then said: "Yeah, we can do that when we get home."

"No, here."

She looked at me longingly. I shot her a look that shut down the longing, and that was that. End of discussion. I had no idea how much I hurt her that day. It wasn't until years later that the hurt came to the surface and was healed.

A lot needed to change in me before that healing could take place.

Sometime after the Holy Spirit revealed to me that the rhythms of Heaven were in the waltz, I was speaking in a conference at a church, where I prayed for anyone who wanted to be prayed for. People crowded around me, and I prayed for everyone I could. A woman stood in the circle, waiting for the touch of God on her life. Somehow in the crush of the crowd, I passed her by. I prayed for one after another after another. The people were so eager; the needs so urgent. I was turning to ones on the right, then on the left, then behind me. Somehow I passed her by again. Still she waited. The third time I passed her, someone saw her, noting the disappointment on her face.

The person tapped my shoulder and whispered in my ear. "You need to pray for her," the person said, pointing to the woman who was about to leave. I motioned her to come forward. By now, she was not only disappointed but angry. I smiled at her and did something I had never done before. "Can we dance?" I asked, extending my arm. And I waltzed with her. We smiled at each other, and I felt the love of God *for* her, the joy of God *in* her, and the oneness He wanted to have *with* her.

By the time we were finished, she had tears in her eyes. Afterward she told me how badly she felt being overlooked. It was the story of her life, she said—overlooked by everyone, including men. And, she felt, overlooked by God. She had left a dance class earlier that night, where she was learning the waltz. She had hoped to meet someone there who might be interested in her, but she left early—overlooked again, rejected again, feeling worthless again. She had come to the service that night to give God one more chance to see if He was interested in her, to see if He was real, to see if He cared. She had decided if He didn't show up in her life that night that she was going to take her life. She, like all of us, longed to belong, longed to be loved, longed to be delighted in, longed to be a part of a family.

The sadness of her story broke my heart.

But the joy on her face broke my sadness.

That night she became the daughter of a big Papa. She put her small hands in His large hands. She put her small feet on His large feet. And they danced a father-daughter dance that was beautiful to behold.

Since then, the Holy Spirit has prompted me to waltz with several other people. In the process, He has been teaching me about the rhythms of Heaven. "Re-ce-ive My love...My love, My love," He seemed to be saying, in time with the beat. "Re-ce-ive My love...My love, My love."

In stepping to the rhythm of the waltz, I realized I could only give away what I had first received. For me, the gesture of leaning back is an image of receiving; leaning forward, an image of giving. The image captures a rhythm of resting to receive, then releasing to give. Lean back in rest, receiving what He has to give me; lean forward in release, giving what I have received to others.

It is first a filling, *then* a spilling. For if we're not filled, we have nothing to give. We're ministering out of our emptiness rather than out of our fullness. A good example of this is found in Ephesians 5:18-19:

And do not be drunk with wine, in which is dissipation; but be filled with the Spirit, speaking to one another in psalms and hymns and spiritual songs, singing and making melody in your heart to the Lord.

First be filled, then empty yourself to others. Receive, then give; rest, then release.

I have come to realize that the Kingdom of God is about receiving, not achieving. Our activity for God is meant to flow rhythmically out of our intimacy with Him. Being "with Him" is how that intimacy is cultivated. Remember what Mark said in his Gospel? Jesus appointed the 12 so that they might be *"with Him"* (Mark 3:14). In the process of following Jesus as closely as they did, the disciples fell in love with Him.

Once that happened, He began to send them out two by two, as partners in the dance (see Mark 6:7).

Since the Holy Spirit revealed to me that the rhythm of Heaven is in the waltz, I have been dancing ever since. And now when I waltz, I often sing in time with the beat: "Re-ce-ive My joy…My joy, My joy. Be-ho-old My child…My child, My child." And the dance goes on—for a minute, for an hour…sometimes two. And sometimes it spills out from the sanctuary…into the foyer…and out to the parking lot.

Six months ago I was in a church in Alabama with my entire family, and after the service I turned to my wife. "Would you like to dance?" She looked shocked. I took her hand, drew her close, and danced with her. Tears filled her eyes, then spilled from her cheeks. Through the tears came healing, wholeness, oneness. Soon she broke down, weeping. My kids, who were watching us from the front row, started weeping, too. Before I knew it, tears swept through the room.

That moment was a taste of Heaven—a taste of the love, the joy, and the unity that awaits us there. A small taste of the family that awaits us there. A brief taste of the home that awaits us there. And that taste—small as it was, brief as it was—both filled me and made me hungry for more.

THE READER'S PRAYER

Papa God,

I can only imagine what all awaits us in Heaven. If You created such a glorious place as the universe, what must our home be like?

If You created all our earthly joys, what must the joys of Heaven be like? Music, feasting, dancing! It's all too wonderful to believe.

To be full of love for everyone as the three of You are full of love for each other.

To be full of joy in everything as the three of You are full of joy in each other.

To be one with each other as the three of You are one with each other.

What an amazing culture exists in Heaven!

What an amazing offer that we can be a part of that culture, that Your Kingdom can come to our lives, here and now; that Your will can be done on earth as it is in Heaven, in my family as well as in the Trinity, in my church here on earth as well as in the culture there in Heaven.

Teach me the rhythm of Heaven, Papa. Draw me close, hold me tight, and whisper in my ear...

Dance, then, wherever you may be,
I am the Lord of the Dance, said He,
And I'll lead you all, wherever you may be,
And I'll lead you all in the Dance, said He.
Sweep me off my feet. Now and forevermore, I pray.

Chapter 3

Seeing God Through the Eyes of His Son

No one has seen God at any time. The only begotten Son, who is in the bosom of the Father, He has declared Him (John 1:18).

Philip said to Him, "Lord, show us the Father, and it is sufficient for us." Jesus said to him, "Have I been with you so long, and yet you have not known Me, Philip? He who has seen Me has seen the Father" (John 14:8-9a).

Jesus came to earth for a number of reasons. The first and foremost reason was to pay the penalty for our sins by dying on the Cross. The second reason was to train disciples to carry on His work after He left. The third was to proclaim the good news of the Kingdom, giving the world a taste of Heaven. Another reason He came, though, was to show us the Father.

Before Jesus came, most people had a distorted picture of God. Some saw Him as an *aloof* God, distant and detached from their everyday lives. Others saw Him as an *authoritarian* God, strict and stern, bringing down His gavel on every transgression, however slight, and mercilessly meting out judgment. Still others saw Him as an *angry* God, prone to fits of rage, fearfully unapproachable.

Jesus came to restore the original picture that had suffered so much damage over the centuries. The composite picture He gave was not of an angry God but of a God whose anger had been appeased through the once-for-all sacrifice that Jesus was sent here to make. The picture He gave was not of an authoritarian God but of an affectionate God. Not of a God who was aloof but of a God who had come near, just as He had come near to Israel in the wilderness to live among them and speak tenderly to them. As God Himself declared, *"I have **tabernacled** in the midst of the sons of Israel, and have become their God"* (Exod. 29:45 YLT).

With the tabernacle, God "pitched His tent," so to speak, in the midst of His people. The blueprints for the tabernacle came from Heaven, and so, when it was finished, it was like having a little bit of Heaven here on earth. The tent was a temporary structure that was pitched in the wilderness, then struck down, packed up, and taken to the next campsite. Its exterior was made with boards and animal skins. Although the outside was humble and plain, the inside was more elaborate, housing the very presence of God. The presence was called the Shekinah glory, a radiant light that was veiled from the congregation so it wouldn't blind them.

The apostle John picked up this image when he wrote the prologue to his Gospel:

> *In the beginning [before all time] was the Word (Christ), and the Word was with God, and the Word was God Himself. ...And the Word (Christ) became flesh (human, incarnate) and **tabernacled** (fixed His tent of flesh, lived awhile) among us; and we [actually] saw His glory (His honor, His majesty), such glory as an only begotten son receives from his father, full of grace (favor, lovingkindness) and truth* (John 1:1,14 AMP).

The tabernacle had no exterior attractiveness that we should be drawn to it; neither did Jesus (see Exod. 26:7; Isa. 53:2). Both were filled with the glory of God, though that glory was veiled (see Exod. 40:34; John 1:14). Here and there, however, that veil was lifted. When Jesus turned the water into wine at the wedding in Cana, for example, John tells us that this was the beginning of signs when Jesus revealed His glory (see John 2:11). With each miracle, a little more of His glory spilled out (see John 4:46-54). One of the greatest revelations of Jesus' glory was at the Mount of Transfiguration, where His face shone like the sun and His garments turned white as light (see Matt. 17:1-8).

In John's Gospel, we learn that Jesus was on a mission to "show and tell"—*telling* us who the Father was, both in stories and in sermons; *showing* us who He was, both in the way Jesus lived and in the way He died. By the time He ascended to Heaven, Jesus had left behind a scrapbook of photographs, full of color and free of distortion, that revealed who God was, along with a sheaf of stories that did the same.

Before we take a look at some of those pictures and listen to some of those stories, I want to talk to you about the whole idea of God as a Father. The gods of pagan religions were petty and capricious, greedy and full of envy, dishonorable and untrustworthy. Never were any of them referred to by the term, *Father*.

Even within Judaism, God is not referred to as the believer's father. He is called *El-Shaddai* (God Almighty; see Gen. 17:1), *Jehovah-Jireh* (the Lord will Provide; see Gen. 22:14), *Jehovah-Rophe* (the Lord Who Heals; see Exod. 15:26), *Jehovah-Sabaoth* (the Lord of Hosts; see 1 Sam. 1:11), *El Elyon* (God Most High; see Genesis 14:18), and other such names. Although God *is* referred to as a *"father of the fatherless"* (Ps. 68:5), He is not referred to as a father to any of the prophets, priests, or patriarchs. He did, however, say He would be a father to David's son, Solomon (see 1 Chron. 22:9-10). Even so, we never hear Solomon addressing God as "Father," almost as if it is too private and too personal for them to say publicly.

For an individual to claim such a relationship would be pretentious at least and blasphemous at most. For example, when Jesus referred to God as *His* Father, note the reaction:

For this reason the Jews were persecuting Jesus, because He was doing these things on the Sabbath. But He answered them, "My Father is working until now, and I Myself am working." For this reason therefore the Jews were seeking all the more to kill Him, because He not only was breaking the Sabbath, but also was calling God His own Father, making Himself equal with God (John 5:16-18 NASB).

Shortly before Jesus preached His first sermon—the Sermon on the Mount—He was baptized in the Jordan. As He came up from the water, God spoke, calling Jesus His beloved Son, which, conversely, meant that God was Jesus' Father. Just two chapters later in Matthew, when Jesus preached His sermon, He used the term *Father* 14 times, referring to God as "your Father" and "our Father." In all, Jesus used the term *Father* to refer to God a total of 149 times in the Gospels—37 times in Matthew, 5 times in Mark, 13 times in Luke, and 94 times in John.

Do you see what Jesus is doing? He is expanding the family circle. Just as the Father longed for sons and daughters, so the Son longed for brothers and sisters. Can you imagine how honored those people felt? If you look at Matthew 4:23-25, you'll see something about those people. So many in the audience that day had been recently healed by Jesus. What a beautiful example of receiving "grace upon grace." First they were restored to their health, to their right minds, to their families, to society. Then they were included in the family of God.

Do you see what else Jesus is doing? He is telling the people that God is entering into a new relationship with them. He will be a Father to *every* one of them. Not just to one favored individual, such as the king, but to every subject within the Kingdom.

If the audience had been from the 21st century, doubtless we would be wondering whether Jesus' words should be taken literally, if they applied to us, what were the implications of "turning the other cheek," and whether that was practical in a fallen world. But for the first-century audience, they would likely all be talking about one thing: "He said *"Father...*'Father'...*'our* Father.' Can you believe it?"

They had never heard anything like it. Not from the scribes. Not from the Pharisees. Not from anyone. When the sermon was over, it wasn't a somber moment, but a celebratory one. Certainly they hugged each other, joy filling their hearts, tears streaming down their faces.

And maybe, just maybe...some of them danced!

A Picture of the Father's Embrace

Now to one of those pictures and one of those stories.

If anyone could *tell* us about the Father, it was Jesus. And, since He was the very image of God and the exact representation of His nature (see Heb. 1:2; Col. 1:15), if anyone could *show* us the Father, it was Jesus. Added to that, Jesus Himself tells us that He only did what He *saw* the Father doing (see John 5:19) and only *spoke* what the Father had taught Him (see John 8:28).

Jesus, of all people, knew what the Father looked like and what He sounded like. John states, *"No one has seen God at any time. The only begotten Son, who is in the bosom of the Father, He has declared Him"* (John 1:18 NASB).

The term *bosom* is used two other places in the New Testament. One of those places is in the parable of the rich man and Lazarus. When the rich man died, he went to a place of torment in Hades, but when Lazarus died, he went to the bosom of Abraham (see Luke 16:22). The other place the figure of speech is used is in the upper room during the Last Supper, where the disciple whom Jesus loved was leaning on Jesus' bosom (see John 13:23).

The Roman mealtime custom of reclining on cushions at low tables was a common practice among the Jews of Jesus' time. To lie next to the host, or to recline "in the bosom" of the host, was an honor reserved for the most favored guest. To be "in the bosom of Abraham" meant to be in the position of greatest honor at the banquet in Heaven. To be in Christ's bosom, the way John was at the Last Supper, marked him as the most favored guest, the one closest to Him and dearest to Him. And so, when John talks about Jesus being *"in the bosom of the Father,"* he is saying that Jesus not only occupies the most favored position but also the most favorable vantage point for describing who the Father is. He was so close to the Father that He could hear His heartbeat.

Another way the word is used is in the context of parents carrying their children (see Isa. 49:22), which brings another image to mind—that of children on the lap of their parent.

> *Then they brought little children to Him, that He might touch them; but the disciples rebuked those who brought them. But when Jesus saw it, He was greatly displeased and said to them, "Let the little children come to Me, and do not forbid them; for of such is the kingdom of God. Assuredly, I say to you, whoever does not receive the kingdom of God as a little child will by no means enter it." And He took them up in His arms, laid His hands on them, and blessed them* (Mark 10:13-16).

This is one of my favorite scenes in the Gospels. When I do conferences, we often include children in the services. Why? Because, Jesus said, *"of such is the kingdom of God."* And if Jesus puts such a high value on them, so should we, don't you think? Most of the time the children are gathered up front between the pulpit and the front row of seats. They sit there, sometimes lie there, and sometimes dance there. We pray over them, touch them, and bless them. More and more we are seeing that the children are having encounters with God. Some of them, while they are soaking in His goodness, talk about going to Heaven and sitting on Jesus' lap. Others talk about seeing angels. Still others draw pictures of what they see when they are in His presence.

Some are healed; all are blessed—and so are all the adults.

But children weren't an integral part of Jewish worship until that day when Jesus elevated them to a position of honor. The scene bustles with excitement. Eager parents, kids in tow, jostling through the crowd, prodding their timid children, then pushing them toward Jesus so He can bless them. The disciples sternly reprimand the parents for the intrusion, because Jesus has more important things to attend to—or so they think. Jesus thinks differently. The text says He was *"greatly displeased"* with His disciples for hindering the children. Once He sets the disciples straight, He waves the children to Him, and they come running. They climb on His lap, sit at His feet, stand by His side. He gathers them in His arms and tousles their hair, smiles at them, asks them their names.

One or two put their heads in His bosom.

In His bosom, they feel honored. On His lap, they feel safe. In His hands, they feel blessed. In His eyes, they feel loved. In His smile, they feel delighted in. And there on His lap, with that squirmy brood of children—so young, so innocent, so trusting—Jesus shows us a picture of the Kingdom of God with its King on His throne. He places the least of these in the position of most honor, gathering them to His bosom and blessing them.

Jesus knew exactly how they felt, and He fought back a nostalgic tear for the bosom of His Father that He had left so many years ago when He climbed down from that lap so we could climb up onto *His.*

A PICTURE OF THE FATHER'S AFFECTION

The Father's lap. Just saying the words conjures up a world of fond associations. That Father is not an angry God...but one whose anger has been appeased. He is not an authoritarian God, full of reprimands...but one who is affectionate, full of blessings. He is not an aloof God...but one who is approachable, even huggable.

The picture of Jesus with the children on His lap is the picture of the Father's posture toward humanity. He is *not* angry. In fact, God is in a good mood, a *very* good mood. Why? Because the problem of sin, which had wreaked havoc on the world for millennia, is about to be dealt a death blow, once and for all. The writer to the Hebrews pictures the Father at peace. In fact, if you trace the words *anger* and *angry* through the Bible, the Old Testament brims with references to God's anger. The New Testament, on the other hand, has only two—both in Hebrews 3, and both referring to God's anger toward the Israelites when they were in the wilderness—from the *Old* Testament.

The Cross is what changed the Father's heart. It is also what broke His heart. And here is the heartrending scene that made the difference.

Before Jesus left this earth to return to the bosom of the Father, He cried out to that Father. The time was late at night; the place, the Garden of Gethsemane. Once there, Jesus walked a little way beyond where He had left Peter, James, and John, then fell to the ground and began praying. The writer to the Hebrews describes the scene as one of anguish, tears, and loud crying (see Heb. 5:7). What Jesus cried out was this: *"Abba! Father! All things are possible for You; remove this cup from Me; yet not what I will, but what You will"* (Mark 14:36 NASB).

The word *abba* is from *ab*, the Hebrew word for father. It is a term of endearment from a young child's first attempt at pronouncing the name *father*. As the child would attempt pronouncing the word *ab,* it would come out "ab-ba." The English equivalent would be "Papa" or "Da-da."

What exactly is going on in that Garden? Jesus is afraid. He is crying, loudly, and for a time, uncontrollably. Suddenly He is a little boy again, climbing onto His Papa's lap, trembling, reaching up, and desperately clinging to His neck. Asking Him—no, *begging* Him—for a reprieve. In essence He pleads, "Papa, please. The cup is too heavy; its contents, too bitter. Do I *have* to take it? *Must* I drink it? Is there *no* other way?"

Though the answer is hard, the lap is soft, and the Father's arms bundle His Son against the chill of night—warming Him, assuring

Him, calming Him. What began in tears, ended in trust. What began as a request, ended as a relinquishment. What began as a way out for the Son, ended as the way of salvation for the world.

All because of the Father's lap.

And because of the Son who sat there, wept there, surrendered there.

The Parable of the Compassionate Father

The clearest and most compelling story that Jesus told to describe the Father can be found in Luke 15:11-32. The reason for telling the story was in response to His critics:

> *Then all the tax collectors and the sinners drew near to Him to hear Him. And the Pharisees and scribes complained, saying, "This Man receives sinners and eats with them"* (Luke 15:1-2).

It wasn't Jesus' first offense. Earlier in Luke, Jesus also responded to His critics: *"The Son of Man has come eating and drinking, and you say, 'Look, a glutton and a winebibber, a friend of tax collectors and sinners'"* (Luke 7:34).

To the scribes and Pharisees, sharing a table with sinners was a sure sign of your acceptance of them. And if you accepted sinners, it was a slippery slope to accepting their sin. Soon the whole religious culture would be in decay.

As these guardians of morality looked on, they began to murmur among themselves: "Look at that! It's disgusting. He's supposed to be a holy man, and look at how He's defiling Himself! He's eating with them, drinking with them, and, worst of all, He seems to be enjoying their company. What a disgrace! He should be corrected. Someone should put Him in His place."

The problem? The religious leaders had a distorted picture of God and of the culture of Heaven.

Jesus corrects both distortions with a story that is not so much about a son as it is about his father. You know the story. The prodigal demands his share of the inheritance. As the indignant older son looks on, the father, remarkably, divides the estate and allows the younger one to leave home.

The story is actually about two prodigals—the prodigal who *left* home…and the prodigal who *stayed* home. The word *prodigal* means "wasteful."[1] There are many ways to waste a life. These sons illustrate two of them. I've tried both. Like the son in the parable, I had a good home. So why did I leave? Like the scribes and Pharisees, I came to have a distorted picture of God and of the culture of Heaven.

This is the story of how those distortions took place and where they took me.

I became a Christian at age 13 in a tiny church in Norway. Shortly afterward, I decided to join its youth group. I came wearing a T-shirt of my school's soccer team. Bad decision. Everyone else in the youth group went to a rival school. As soon as I arrived, the group started taunting me. The boys jumped me, wrestling me to the ground. The girls stood by and watched, laughing. They finally ripped off my shirt and tore it to shreds.

I left, humiliated and determined. If this is what Jesus and His Father are like, I'm going to throw in my lot with the devil. I smoked my first hashish at 13. After that, I tried everything—drugs, alcohol, sex. I was arrested at 15. By 18, I tried to kill myself.

I had to get away, leave home, leave town. My parents arranged for me to go to boarding school. I drove alone from the west coast of Norway to the east coast, and threw what little I had into my dorm room. It didn't take long to find a new supplier. Once I did, I was in business, buying and selling drugs.

Until one day when a police car screeched into the parking lot outside my room.

I ran.

My photo and alleged crimes were plastered over the newspapers, bringing shame and heartache to my family. With nowhere to go, I lived on the streets, loitering among the shadows, turning my collar to the cold, ducking into alleyways to avoid being spotted. Finally I went to Oslo, where I thought the big city could hide me. There I found myself in the dark labyrinth of the drug world. These were serious addicts, not recreational users. They were mean streets, in Oslo. Hard, cold, lonely, and violent.

I no longer knew who God was. All I knew was that He wasn't safe. He wasn't there to protect me, either from the youth culture at church or from the drug culture on the street.

The streets got meaner and dirtier. I couldn't remember the last time I had bathed. My clothes stank. My hair was long and filthy. Full of shame, full of fear, I stayed drugged up. It was the only way I could survive—until survival no longer mattered. Once again, I was suicidal.

I had hit rock bottom, just like the prodigal son in the story. What turned him around was the same thing that turned me around—a picture of home.

> But when he came to himself, he said, "How many of my father's hired servants have bread enough and to spare, and I perish with hunger! I will arise and go to my father, and will say to him, 'Father, I have sinned against heaven and before you, and I am no longer worthy to be called your son. Make me like one of your hired servants'" (Luke 15:17-19).

Home. I missed it so much. Missed *Mor's* [Norwegian for "mother"] love, her cooking. Missed *Far* [Norwegian for "father"] sitting in his chair, reading the newspaper. Missed my brother, too, and my sister. Missed my room, my bed. A hot bath. A full refrigerator.

I made the phone call.

I would take the train, I told him. He would meet me at the station, he said. For two and a half hours, the train clacked over the rails. I was so glad to be going home and, at the same time, so scared. I had let down everyone I loved. I didn't know how they would respond. I didn't know what to say, how to act. I tried rehearsing some sort of confession, like the one the prodigal son came up with. But I got nothing. The closer the train came to home, the more anxious I became.

When the train pulled into the station, I got off, tentatively, looking around. And then I saw him. *Far*. Running to me. I fought back tears. When he reached me, we fell into each other's arms, both of us crying. I had seen him cry only twice in his life, and one of those times was for me.

For me!

As I recall this picture, another picture comes to mind:

And he arose and came to his father. But when he was still a great way off, his father saw him and had compassion, and ran and fell on his neck and kissed him (Luke 15:20).

I'm not sure what I said. "I'm sorry," I am sure. But besides that, I don't remember. Nor do I remember what we said on the way home. When we got there, my *far* opened the door, revealing my whole family, cheering me, hugging me, crying with me.

My 15-year-old brother was a caterer at the time and had made this wonderful marzipan cake with a scrawl of frosted words: *Velkommen Hjem, Leif!*

Welcome Home, Leif!

They loved on me and said things like, "You are family! We love you! We believe in you!"

And as I recall that scene, another comes to mind:

But the father said to his servants, "Bring out the best robe and put it on him, and put a ring on his hand and sandals on his feet. And

bring the fatted calf here and kill it, and let us eat and be merry;
for this my son was dead and is alive again; he was lost and is
found." And they began to be merry (Luke 15:22-24).

The good news: I came home to my family and home to God.

The bad news: I went to church.

GOING FROM PRODIGAL TO PHARISEE

I went from being filled with pleasures in the distant country to
being filled with pride in my father's fields. Like the dutiful older brother,
I was diligent in my chores. I studied, I prayed, I worked. I went to
church, to meetings, and more meetings. I wanted to pay for my sins—
do some kind of Protestant penance to absolve my guilt. I wanted to be
holy, which, in my mind, meant to do more and sin less.

I went to Bible college, where I studied more, prayed more, worked
more. Then I went to seminary, where I studied harder, prayed harder,
worked harder. Finally I got my first church and my first and only family. The only problem was that they weren't *doing* enough. The people in
the church weren't doing enough. My wife wasn't doing enough. My kids
weren't doing enough. Of course, I didn't feel *I* was doing enough either.

I was on this hamster wheel, running as hard as I could. Although
the wheel was turning faster and faster, I was getting nowhere. Nowhere
in my relationship with God—and nowhere in my relationship with anyone else.

I was living just like the older son in the story (see Luke 15:25-30).
Like him, I felt overworked and underappreciated. And like him, I was
angry. Angry at my congregation for not pulling their weight. Angry at
my wife, my kids. And angry at God.

I had taken two very different paths over the years. One led to rebellion; the other, to religion. Both led away from home, away from joy, and
away from the Father's heart.

From 1984 until 2000, I worked my Father's fields from sunup to sundown. I plowed furrow after furrow. I planted, I weeded, I watered. But after 16 years, I was worn out.

There must be a better way, I thought.

There *must* be.

THE READER'S PRAYER

Abba, Father.

Thank You for sending Your dearly beloved Son not only to save us but to show us who You are.

And who You are is wonderful!

Thank You for all the pictures and the stories that Jesus left for us to look at and to love.

To learn what You are like, all we have to do is look at His pictures and listen to His stories.

And what do they show us, what do they tell us?

That You are a Father upon whose lap we can crawl, at whose feet we can play, at whose side we can stand.

That You are there to bless us, not berate us.

That You are never too busy for us.

Thank You for a Father's lap that offers a place to so many children, and thank You for a Father's love that reaches out to so many prodigals.

But most of all, Papa, most of all...thank You for Your home, and for making so much room in it for all of us, Your children.

PART 2

SEEING OURSELVES THE WAY THE FATHER SEES US

God in Christ is not condemner but Redeemer ("God sent His Son into the world not to condemn the world but that the world might be saved through Him"). We in Christ are not the condemned but the redeemed, not the pimply Adam but the "all fair" Bride. That's the Gospel, the good news that's too good to be true yet is true. Not to believe it is to believe even the more unbelievable bad news that God is a liar. God is either a lover or a liar. –Peter Kreeft[1]

CHAPTER 4

SEEING MAN IN HIS GLORY AND PARADISE IN ITS SPLENDOR

O LORD, our Lord, how majestic is Your name in all the earth, who have displayed Your splendor above the heavens! From the mouth of infants and nursing babes You have established strength because of Your adversaries, to make the enemy and the revengeful cease. When I consider Your heavens, the work of Your fingers, the moon and the stars, which You have ordained; what is man that You take thought of him, and the son of man that You care for him? (Psalm 8:1-4 NASB).

MAN IN HIS GLORY

After 16 years of serving God, I felt like the critical older brother in the Parable of the Prodigal Son. I was fairly self-righteous, easily irritated, often resentful, and sometimes angry. Although I was in crisis, I didn't know it at the time. It wasn't until I received the "baptism of love" (which I talk about in Chapter 6), that I even realized what the crisis was or how bad it was.

The crisis, at its root, was an *identity* crisis. I didn't know who I was—and if you don't know who you are, that confusion will follow you everywhere, affecting everything. Every meal with your family. Every meeting with your co-workers. Every moment of every day, down to your quiet time.

The two most important questions a person can ask are "Who am I?" and "Why am I here?" In spite of my college education, my seminary training, and my pastoral experience, I wasn't sure I could answer those questions. All I knew was that my search for significance had left me empty-handed and empty-hearted. I had been running on that emptiness for a long time. And I couldn't do it anymore. I just couldn't.

One of the things I learned in my search was that *alignment always precedes assignment.* Once you are aligned with your God-given identity, you are ready for your God-given assignment.

We live in a culture that has lost its collective identity, and that is because we, as members of that culture, have lost our *individual* identities. I'm not talking abstractly. I'm talking about you and me, about your family and mine, your church and my church.

Our culture worships at the Pantheon of Marketable Images—from Hollywood to Madison Avenue, from MTV to ESPN, from billboards on the highway to magazines at the grocery store. That is where we get our images of what it means to be a man, what it means to be a woman, what it means to be a teenager. If we align ourselves with those images, everything else will be out of alignment.

It's nothing less than identity theft on a grand scale.

So where do we go to get our identities back?

The fifth-century Greek philosopher, Protagoras, said we go to ourselves; "Man is the measure of all things," he is famous for saying. We ourselves are the standard by which all things are understood, defined, and valued. But that view only raises more questions. Even if we agree with him, *which* man do we select to do the measuring—an Albert Schweitzer or an Adolph Hitler? The yardsticks of each would be vastly different. If we begin with man and his natural eyes—regardless of *which* man—we are liable to lose our bearings and end up lost in the cosmos.

So where *do* we begin?

We begin "in the beginning" with God, which is where David began. He looked up. And when he saw the vast, heavenly expanse, it was impossible for him to come to the same conclusion Protagoras did. Instead, he couldn't imagine why God would care for something so small and insignificant as a human being: *"What is man that You take thought of him,"* David asked, *"and the son of man that You care for him?"* (Ps. 8:4 NASB).

But the One who gave the stars to awe us, gave the Scriptures to awe us even more. In the second part of Psalm 8, David reflects on the biblical account of Creation, which reveals exactly who you and I are and why we are here:

> *Yet You have made him a little lower than God, and You crown him with glory and majesty! You make him to rule over the works of Your hands; You have put all things under his feet, all sheep and oxen, and also the beasts of the field, the birds of the heavens and the fish of the sea, whatever passes through the paths of the seas. O LORD, our Lord, how majestic is Your name in all the earth!* (Psalm 8:5-9 NASB).

You and I are made not a little higher than animals. Not a little lower than angels. We are made a little lower *than God*. Can you believe it? *Do* you believe it? If you and I are clear about our identity, we will *also* take it with us to every meal with our family, every meeting with our co-workers, every moment of every day, down to our quiet time. That identity will affect everything. Imagine if we saw our children as a little lower than God. Imagine if we saw our mate that way, the receptionist at work, the checker at the grocery store. How would it affect the way we think about that person, how we talk with that person, and, more importantly, how we listen?

If that isn't enough to awe you, look at the second half of that verse. God *crowns* us. We are royalty, you and I. And so are our children, our mate, the receptionist, the checker. What does God crown us *with*? Glory and majesty! *Whose* glory and *whose* majesty? *His!* He shares not just His work but His glory, not just His authority but His majesty. Can you believe it? God has chosen you and me to be partakers of the very characteristics He has displayed in creation, and they sparkle like jewels in our crowns.

Get ready for the Scriptures to awe you even more. Go back to the book of beginnings—Genesis—and see where David came to his conclusions about who we are and why we are here.

At first glance, the creation stories in Genesis 1 and 2 seem at odds with each other. Some critics have gone so far as to say that they are two separate accounts, written by two different authors.

The problem is easily resolved, however, if you see chapter 1 as the panoramic view, fitting in all six days of creation, and chapter 2 as a close-up, focusing on the sixth day when Adam and Eve were created. One gives us a sequential picture, set in time; the other gives us a spatial picture, set in place. Seen as such, the two chapters are not contradictory but complementary.

With that overview, let's take a closer look at man in his glory.

Then God said, "Let Us make man in Our image, according to Our likeness; let them have dominion over the fish of the sea, over the birds of the air, and over the cattle, over all the earth and over every creeping thing that creeps on the earth." So God created man in His own image; in the image of God He created him; male and female He created them. Then God blessed them, and God said to them, "Be fruitful and multiply; fill the earth and subdue it; have dominion over the fish of the sea, over the birds of the air, and over every living thing that moves on the earth" (Genesis 1:26-28).

Here again is an example of how alignment precedes assignment. The man and woman are shown their worth before they are shown their work. They are given their identities before they are given their responsibilities.

The first thing that jumps out of the text is the personal and possessive pronouns, "us" and "our." The picture is of the Father, the Son, and the Holy Spirit deliberating with one another about the decision to create man. There is no rancor in Their deliberations, no political maneuvering, no greed about who will own the patent, no selfishness about who will receive the credit. This is a discussion among equals. There is a diversity of roles but a unity of relationship with mutual honor and mutual respect. There is such love and joy and harmony within the Trinity that it would be unthinkable, if not impossible, for one to upstage the other.

So great is the love, the joy, and the unity among Themselves that They needed a universe to hold and display it all. But amid the glories of the universe, They needed a special representative who would both bear that image and display that image.

The words *image* and *likeness* are two very picturesque words in the text. *Likeness* is used in Scripture to refer to a replica or copy of something. In Second Kings 16:10, for example, Ahaz made a copy of Tiglath-pileser's altar in Damascus. *Image* is used in Scripture to refer to a statue.[1] In Daniel 3:1-7, for instance, Nebuchadnezzar made an impressive image of himself and placed it in the plain of Dura so that all could see it and worship it. In the ancient East, the king over the land would place a statue of himself to proclaim his dominion of the territory where the statue was erected. All who lived in that territory were subject to his rule. In a similar way, God placed an image of Himself in the plain of Eden, proclaiming His reign over that territory.

Bill Johnson, in his book, *When Heaven Invades Earth,* describes the process:

The backbone of Kingdom authority and power is found in the *commission*. Discovering God's original commission and purpose for mankind can help us fortify our resolve to a life of history changing significance. To find that truth we must go back to the beginning.

Man was created in the image of God and placed into the Father's ultimate expression of beauty and peace: the Garden of Eden. Outside of that garden it was a different story. It was without the order and blessing contained within and was in great need of the touch of God's delegated one—Adam.

Adam and Eve were placed in the garden with a mission. God said, "Be fruitful and multiply; fill the earth and subdue it." It was God's intention that as they bore more children, who also lived under God's rule, they would be extending the boundaries of His garden (His government) through the simplicity of their devotion to Him. The greater the number of people in right relationship to God, the greater the impact of their leadership. The process would continue until the entire earth was covered with the glorious rule of God through man.[2]

The text in Genesis tells us that God made man like a sculptor makes a statue out of clay. But in this case, the artist breathes into the work of art, giving it life. Imagine the first moment of consciousness. The first face that Adam sees is his Father's face. The first voice he hears is his Father's voice. The first touch he feels is his Father's touch. The first love he feels is his Father's love. The first joy he feels is the Father's delight.

Many think that Adam was created in the garden, but the text of Genesis says otherwise: *"The LORD God planted a garden eastward in Eden, and there He put the man whom He had formed"* (Gen. 2:8).

How long he waited for God to show him his new home, we aren't told. But most certainly it took a while. And all the while, Adam was waiting and wondering, his eyes adjusting to everything that was fresh and new. I think God wanted to surprise him and give him the garden as a gift. Like fixing up the nursery before the baby comes home from the hospital, making it warm and cozy, calming and inviting.

But God had another surprise in mind—an even greater gift than the Garden of Eden!

THE FEMININE SIDE OF GOD

In Genesis 1:27, the text says: *"So God created man in His own image; in the image of God He created him; male and female He created them."* What is intriguing in this passage is that the image of God is made up of both male and female components. There is a masculine side of God, with which we are all familiar. But there is also a feminine side.

The Scriptures use both masculine and feminine images to describe who God is and how He relates to us. In Isaiah 49:14-15, for example, the image used to describe God's relationship with us is that of a mother to her nursing child. In Matthew 23:37, another image is used, that of a mother hen gathering her chicks under her wings.

Even though the masculine pronoun is always used of God, along with masculine attributes, such as Father, there are some decidedly feminine characteristics of God that sometimes jar us. One of these is in the Parable of the Prodigal Son. The decision to let the younger son leave is more of a masculine response to a rebellious child. But when the son returns, the father's actions are more of a feminine response. He runs to the boy, showers him with kisses and hugs, gets him fresh clothes, and throws a party for him.

Turning to the text of Genesis, we see some important words that describe the woman and her relationship to man: *"And the LORD God said, 'It is not good that man should be alone; I will make him a **helper** comparable to him'"* (Gen. 2:18).

We will consider the word *helper*. Traditionally, this has been interpreted as the woman being a kind of a personal assistant. But the word is so much richer than that. The Hebrew word for "helper" is used around 80 times in the Old Testament. Two things characterize the word. One, it is used primarily in military contexts. And two, it is used primarily of God. The word has essentially the same meaning in all the languages that are related to the Hebrew. It means "to rescue" or "to save." It is used of a military ally who comes to fight beside us when we come under attack, which is how the word is used in Psalm 46:4-6:

> *There is a river whose streams shall make glad the city of God, the holy place of the tabernacle of the Most High. God is in the midst of her, she shall not be moved; God shall **help** her, just at the break of dawn. The nations raged, the kingdoms were moved; He uttered His voice, the earth melted.*

It is interesting that right after the creation of the woman is the first attack by the enemy in chapter 3. Regrettably, both were ignorant of his strategies, both were untried in battle, and both failed each other.

There is a beautiful scene at the end of the movie *What Women Want* that illustrates the usage of "helper" as a "rescuer." After a failure of character, the male lead confesses his failing to his female co-star. At that moment, the actress must make a critical decision. Do I reject him or rescue him? She decides to do the noble thing, the knightly thing. She saves his job, their relationship, and rescues him from his own selfishness. Often, that is how a woman rescues a man—from himself. From the side of himself that is distant or distracted, from the side of himself that is task-oriented instead of people-oriented, from the side of himself that would rather watch football on television than play football in the backyard with his kids. In doing so, she helps him to become a better father, a better friend, a better son, a better man.

So much of my ministry is across the country and around the world, on the front lines of the spiritual war. That is my assignment. But I could never do that assignment if my wife Jennifer's assignment wasn't the home front. I can leave home because I know that she is there fighting the everyday battles with car wrecks and teenage heartaches, mailing our prayer requests and meeting with repairmen. She rescues me from my biggest enemy—myself! She knows that the responsibilities I face are often overwhelming. She also knows that I feel too guilty sometimes to take the time to do something that might ease the stress and relax me. She gives me the permission to be selfish, in the best sense of the word. She knows that a stressed Leif is not a good thing to have around the house, and she knows that by taking care of myself, I am taking care of her and the kids.

The other word in Genesis 2:18 that sheds light on the woman is *comparable*. The word means "suitable for" or "corresponding to." It pictures something being put before someone, face to face, so that the similarities and differences can be easily seen. Picture corresponding pieces of a puzzle or a lock and key, and you get a good idea of the meaning of the word.

> *Out of the ground the* Lord *God formed every beast of the field and every bird of the air, and brought them to Adam to see what he would call them. And whatever Adam called each living creature, that was its name. So Adam gave names to all cattle, to the birds of the air, and to every beast of the field. But for Adam there was not found a helper* **comparable** *to him* (Genesis 2:19-20).

As the animals paraded by Adam, he saw that they were paired according to their kind, but with one significant difference. They were made to fit within each other, like interlocking pieces of a puzzle. After a while, it must have become frustrating for Adam to realize that he had no companion whose similarities corresponded to his and whose differences complemented his. Something was missing, and he ached to find it.

Again, there is a great illustration of this from a movie. *Jerry Maguire* is a story about a sports agent who is "good at friendship but bad at intimacy." He finally marries, but he realizes that he doesn't know how to share his life with a woman, let alone his soul. They separate, but, when he sees another couple madly in love, it accentuates his aloneness, and he aches for the missing part of himself that his wife carries. He returns to fight for her, telling her that she "completes" him. That is the sense of the word that describes the woman in Genesis 2.

When a man realizes his incompleteness, it humbles him. In humbling him, it makes him vulnerable to grace. And in that state, wonderful things happen.

> *And the LORD God caused a deep sleep to fall on Adam, and he slept; and He took one of his ribs, and closed up the flesh in its place. Then the rib which the LORD God had taken from man He made into a woman, and He brought her to the man. And Adam said: "This is now bone of my bones and flesh of my flesh; she shall be called Woman, because she was taken out of Man." Therefore a man shall leave his father and mother and be joined to his wife, and they shall become one flesh. And they were both naked, the man and his wife, and were not ashamed* (Genesis 2:21-25).

Here again is a replication of the Trinity. You have the lover, the beloved, and the spirit of love moving between them—mutual love, mutual joy, mutual oneness. I think of all these things, and I think of my wife Jennifer. I think of all the ways she has been my ally, all the ways she has completed me, and I am overwhelmed by the goodness of God in giving her to me.

She balances me, and that is one of the ways she completes me. I'm like a kite, eager to catch the next gust of wind. I love living like that. The views are fantastic! But someone has to hold my kite strings to keep me from flying into the power lines. And someone eventually has to bring me down to earth. She does that for me. I am a dreamer; she is the practical one. And that is another way she balances me, completing me. I have an adventurous spirit; she is more of a homebody. I am almost fearless when it comes to taking risks; she makes sure that if I jump at one of those risks that I at least have a parachute on.

The next section deals with Paradise in its splendor, and when I think of that, I realize how hard my wife works to make our home an Eden. I am gone an average of 250 days a year. I stay at a lot of nice places, eat at a lot of nice restaurants, visit with a lot of nice people, but I'm here to tell you: "There's no place like home." There's no place like your own bed to sleep in. There's no food like your wife's cooking. And there's no sound as sweet as the voices in your own family, especially when they laugh. Jennifer loves to cook, and because of that, the house is always filled with the smell of something delicious baking in the oven. And she is almost always in the kitchen, making something, serving someone, laughing with someone. Half of the goodness of her food is the love she puts into it. I'm not kidding, you can taste it. I love that she gives everyone in our family their own space. I love how she knows how much space each of us needs, and she is always careful to respect that space.

For me, there's *no place* like home. And the biggest reason is because there's *no person* like Jennifer—my friend, my ally, my everything.

PARADISE IN ITS SPLENDOR

The Garden of Eden has always fascinated me, both as a young boy and as an adult. The biblical passage that describes it is short and simply written.

The LORD God planted a garden eastward in Eden, and there He put the man whom He had formed. And out of the ground the LORD God made every tree grow that is pleasant to the sight and good for food. The tree of life was also in the midst of the garden, and the tree of the knowledge of good and evil. Now a river went out of Eden to water the garden, and from there it parted and became four riverheads. The name of the first is Pishon; it is the one which skirts the whole land of Havilah, where there is gold. And the gold of that land is good. Bdellium and the onyx stone are there. The name of the second river is Gihon; it is the one which goes around the whole land of Cush. The name of the third river is

Hiddekel; it is the one which goes toward the east of Assyria. The fourth river is the Euphrates. Then the LORD God took the man and put him in the garden of Eden to tend and keep it (Genesis 2:8-15).

The description reads like a pirate map with a bold X that marks the spot of buried treasure. In this case, the spot is a garden in the land of Eden. *Eden* itself is a cryptic word with disputed origins. Some scholars believe it is derived from a Hebrew verb, meaning "to luxuriate," as it is used in Nehemiah 9:25. The noun form would therefore mean "a luxury" or "a delight," and this is how the word is used in Psalm 36:8. Other scholars believe the word originated from the Sumerians. Sumer was the Mesopotamian region that produced the world's first written language, and their word *eden* meant "a fertile plain."[3]

Regardless of the derivation, though, the Genesis text gives a few clues of what that garden was like. First, it was designed by God, the grand Architect of the universe, so that should tell us something. He was also the one who implemented the design. He was both the landscape architect, who did the design, and the laborer, who did the digging. So you know that the garden was not only well planned but well planted.

Some of the great gardens of the world were designed by a man named Frederick Law Olmstead, recognized as the "founder of American landscape architecture."[4] One of his achievements was designing and overseeing the landscape plan for the Biltmore House, the largest private residence in the U.S., owned by George Vanderbilt, with an original estate of 120,000 acres.

His most noted achievement, though, was Central Park in New York City, which he designed with English architect, Calvert Vaux. The foliage in the park appears natural, but it was almost entirely landscaped. The park contains several lakes and ponds, extensive walking and bridle trails, a zoo, a wildlife sanctuary, a kaleidoscope of flowers, shrubs, and ground cover, along with a forest of over 25,000 trees. It sits like an Eden in the midst of the cold steel and gray concrete of the city.

Imagine this. Imagine the landscape architect not being a man, however talented, but an almighty God. Imagine the funds for the project not coming from the coffers of men, however rich, but from the inexhaustible riches of Heaven. Image what kind of garden *that* would be. Imagine the most beautiful garden you have ever seen. Do you see it in your mind's eye? Now realize that it is merely a vestige of Eden.

So what *did* that unspoiled garden look like?

Here and there in the Scriptures we are given glimpses of that "garden of delights." The glimpses are few and fleeting, but they are breathtaking in their beauty and beguiling in their enchantment. Here's one of those glimpses in Isaiah 51:3:

For the LORD will comfort Zion, He will comfort all her waste places; He will make her wilderness like Eden, and her desert like the garden of the LORD; joy and gladness will be found in it, thanksgiving and the voice of melody.

Imagine a time when you were the happiest, when you were filled with "joy and gladness." Do you see it? Now realize that that joy was a mere vestige of Eden. Imagine the most enchanting music you have ever heard. Do you hear it? Now realize that that music was a distant and distorted echo of a melody floating on a breeze that flowed through Eden's trees.

In a prophecy from Ezekiel, the exiled Jews in Babylon are given a vision of their restored temple, and again, the vision is merely a vestige of Eden.

Along the bank of the river, on this side and that, will grow all kinds of trees used for food; their leaves will not wither, and their fruit will not fail. They will bear fruit every month, because their water flows from the sanctuary. Their fruit will be for food, and their leaves for medicine (Ezekiel 47:12).

The image is of the trees in Eden, magical by today's standards. Specifically, the image of the tree of life is alluded to, known for its powers to heal. We sometimes skip over shopworn passages like that because we are so familiar with them. But think about it: a tree of life with healing properties, offering life everlasting, maturity without senility. No disease. No decay. No death. It seems something out of a fairy tale—except it's no fairy tale. Once upon a time, there really was such a place.

Imagine a time when you were the strongest and healthiest and the most alive you have ever felt. Now realize that those feelings are only a vague sensation of what was once Eden.

We get another glimpse of Eden in Ezekiel 28:12-14, which is reminiscent of the gold and precious stones from the passage in Genesis 2 (see also Rev. 21:11-22). Speaking to the King of Tyre, a reflection of satan, Ezekiel writes,

You were the seal of perfection, full of wisdom and perfect in beauty. You were in Eden, the garden of God; every precious stone was your covering: the sardius, topaz, and diamond, beryl, onyx, and jasper, sapphire, turquoise, and emerald with gold. (Ezekiel 28:12b-13a)

Imagine dawn in Eden: the morning sun sends shafts of light across the misty meadows, and the grass literally sparkles. Then you rub your eyes, and you realize that the shimmering you see is not dewdrops...but *gemstones*!

That was Eden. No wonder it is called a garden of delights. In that garden there was no crisis of identity, no confusion of responsibility. Our first parents were sacred—sharing together the very image of God. And their lives were significant—sharing together the valuable work of God.

We all have a need for significance. Besides survival, it is the strongest drive we have. We need to know that our life matters, that who we are and why we are here counts for something.

So. *Who* are you? And *why* are you here?

You are God's crowning achievement, His *masterpiece*. You were fearfully and wonderfully made. You were also *purposefully* made. You are here for a reason—to bear God's image and to establish His heavenly Kingdom here on earth.

You are a co-creator with Him, a co-ruler with Him, and a co-lover with Him. He has hand-picked you to expand the boundaries of Eden. He has chosen you to dance in step with the Trinity—embracing those around you and bringing them into the circle where the family of God loves one another, rejoices in one another, and lives in harmony with one another.

In this vast and expansive universe, you matter.

You!

You are loved beyond comprehension.

You are precious beyond words.

You are valued beyond measure.

Just before I started writing this book, I was on my back for five days straight. During that time, my Papa kept whispering in my ear: "I am good, and you are very, very valuable."

That's all. Those same words, over and over again, for *five* days! You would think I would have grown tired of hearing it. I didn't. Just the opposite, in fact. It was music to my ears.

Why did He keep repeating it? I wondered.

I think because it is part of my alignment. And maybe the whole of my assignment, at least for this part of my life—to tell people about the goodness of God and to remind them how valuable they are.

Because sometimes I forget how good God really is and how crazy He is about me.

Sometimes we *all* forget.

THE READER'S PRAYER

Dear Father in Heaven,

Thank You for the stars strewn across the night sky, telling of Your glory; and for the Scriptures stretched across my morning lap, telling me of mine.

Thank You for the dignity of being made in Your image, crowned with glory and majesty.

Help me to bear that image honorably and to wear that crown humbly.

Help me to see who I am and why I am here.

Align me, Lord, before You assign me.

Show me how to cultivate Edens all around me—whether at home or at work, at school or in my small group, so I might bring something of Heaven to earth, something of Heaven's culture to my culture.

May the rich abundance of life You have entrusted to me teach me, whether that life is a growing family or a country garden of friends.

Teach me to work humbly, on my knees.

Teach me to work lovingly, caring for all that tender growth.

Teach me to work joyfully, surrounded by such fragrant reminders of who You are.

Teach me to work gently, both in planting seeds and in pulling weeds.

Teach me to work harmoniously, careful not to trample the worth of the one beside me.

Please know how grateful I am, Lord, for the beauty that blooms all around me, and for the bounty that hangs so heavy on the branches.

Grant me the eyes to see it, my Father, and the heart to appreciate it.

CHAPTER 5

SEEING PARADISE LOST AND OUR HOMESICKNESS FOR EDEN

Then the LORD God said, "Behold, the man has become like one of Us, to know good and evil. And now, lest he put out his hand and take also of the tree of life, and eat, and live forever"— therefore the LORD God sent him out of the garden of Eden to till the ground from which he was taken. So He drove out the man; and He placed cherubim at the east of the garden of Eden, and a flaming sword which turned every way, to guard the way to the tree of life (Genesis 3:22-24).

Imagine for a moment what it was like to live in Paradise.

The perfect neighborhood, perfect home.

The perfect body, perfect health.

The perfect mate, perfect relationship.

The perfect job, perfect provision.

Perfect love, perfect joy, perfect unity.

And, the perfect church—a choir composed of songbirds, the stained-glass beauty of the morning sun filtering through green leaves and colorful blossoms, a magnificent sanctuary with climate-controlled temperature, soft cushions of grass, and the fragrance of flowers all around you. Best of all, the greatest of preachers—God Himself—teaching you, counseling you, caring for you.

What could possibly go wrong?

PARADISE LOST

To find out what went wrong we have to go back to Eden, to the original conversation God had with Adam.

> *Then the LORD God took the man and put him in the garden of Eden to tend and keep it. And the LORD God commanded the man, saying, "Of every tree of the garden you may freely eat; but of the tree of the knowledge of good and evil you shall not eat, for in the day that you eat of it you shall surely die"* (Genesis 2:15-17).

God offered Adam the abundance of Eden. Of *every* tree he could *freely* eat. There was one restriction, and *only* one. He couldn't eat of the tree of the knowledge of good and evil. Why? He was not told. He was only told that it would be harmful to him. How harmful? Fatally.

Remember, Eve has not yet been created, and so we must infer that Adam communicated God's words to her. To see how well those words were communicated, we have to jump forward to Eve's encounter with the serpent:

> *Now the serpent was more cunning than any beast of the field which the LORD God had made. And he said to the woman, "Has God indeed said, 'You shall not eat of every tree of the garden'?" And the woman said to the serpent, "We may eat the fruit of the trees of the garden; but of the fruit of the tree which is in the midst of the garden, God has said, 'You shall not eat it, nor shall you touch it, lest you die.'" Then the serpent said to the woman, "You will not surely die. For God knows that in the day you eat of it your eyes will be opened, and you will be like God, knowing good and*

evil." So when the woman saw that the tree was good for food, that it was pleasant to the eyes, and a tree desirable to make one wise, she took of its fruit and ate. She also gave to her husband with her, and he ate (Genesis 3:1-6).

The serpent, we are told elsewhere in the Scriptures, is none other than satan himself (see Rev. 12:9). Also elsewhere in Scripture we are told that it was satan's cunning that made the deception possible (see 2 Cor. 11:3). Paul tells us that we should not be ignorant of his schemes (see 2 Cor. 2:11). A closer look at the Genesis account reveals some of those schemes.

The devil's first tactic is to disguise who he is (see 2 Cor. 11:14). He transforms himself into one of the animals that God had created—certainly one that Adam was familiar with, having named the animals, and most likely one that Eve was familiar with, because she wasn't the least bit surprised by seeing it.

The devil's second tactic is to divide and conquer. He doesn't go against the couple in a frontal assault. Instead he confronts Eve. Why? Because the commandment had been given to Adam. He passed it on to Eve, whose grasp of it was less certain—and we know this by the way she answers the serpent's questions.

The devil's third tactic is to cast a shadow of doubt on the words of God. "Has God *indeed* said?" In other words, "You weren't there, were you? I mean...when God gave the command. Are you sure you heard it right?" The devil goes on to refresh her memory, subtly paraphrasing. *"You shall not eat of every tree of the garden,'* is that what He said?" Eve corrects him with a more accurate and more positive version: *"We may eat the fruit of the trees of the garden."* Look closely at what is happening. God told Adam that they could eat *freely* from *every* tree. In her version, though, she minimizes the freedom that God had given them. Then, in her next breath, she maximizes the restriction: *"But of the fruit of the tree which is in the midst of the garden, God has said, 'You shall not eat it, nor shall you touch it, lest you die.'"* God never said not to touch it; only not to eat it. Finally, she minimizes the consequence of disobeying the command. She says that God said, *"lest you die."* What He actually said was, *"you shall **surely** die."* Either Adam did a poor job communicating what God had told him, or else Eve did a poor job listening. Even so, he could have spoken up. He *should* have spoken up. But he remained silent.

The devil's fourth and final tactic is to call God's character and His motives into question: "You will not surely die. For God knows that in the day you eat of it your eyes will be opened, and you will be like God, knowing good and evil."

"God lied to you," the serpent brashly declared. "And what kind of a god would do *that*? There must be a motive, and likely an ulterior one. He knows something you *don't* know. And I'm going to let you in on the secret. God is afraid of you because He knows the power of the tree. You're a lot like God, but not *just* like God. I mean, look at the arrangement. *You* work for *Him*. He calls the shots. He tells you what to do and what not to do, what to eat and what not to eat. Where is all this leading? Who knows what restrictions will be next? Do you really want to live like that, your life under His thumb, for the rest of your life? Or do you want to be the one in control? You can have it all. It's yours for the taking. All you have to do is reach out…"

So when the woman saw that the tree was good for food, that it was pleasant to the eyes, and a tree desirable to make one wise, she took of its fruit and ate. She also gave to her husband with her, and he ate (Genesis 3:6).

The consequences were tragic in their severity and cosmic in their scope. At the moment when Adam and Eve took the forbidden fruit, the universe experienced a cataclysm. Theologians refer to it as "the Fall." From the epicenter of Eden, tremors of that Fall were felt to the farthest star, shaking everything, unsettling everything.

Paradise would be lost.

And so much more than Paradise.

LOVE IN THE MISSION

It is hard for a child to see all the love behind a parent's discipline, but, if you have ever raised children, you know it is there. In fact, we are told in Scripture that not only is God's love behind the discipline but that the discipline is proof of our sonship (see Heb. 12:5-11).

Love is everywhere you look in the Genesis passage. You just have to have the right eyes to see it. Let's first look at something we overlooked. Go back and look at the mission God gave to Adam and Eve, but look at it through Heaven's eyes.

The mission comes in two parts. The first part is recorded in Genesis 1:28:

Then God blessed them, and God said to them, "Be fruitful and multiply; fill the earth and subdue it; have dominion over the fish of the sea, over the birds of the air, and over every living thing that moves on the earth."

The second part is recorded in Genesis 2:15: *"Then the Lord God took the man and put him in the garden of Eden to tend and keep it."*

Adam and Eve were to fill the earth with their offspring, subdue the earth with their dominion, and cultivate the earth with their labor. God's love was behind it all and in it all, moving out from it all to reach Adam and Eve. God in His love gave the couple the enjoyment of sex and the fulfillment of procreation. They were able to share in something that was a beautiful image of the oneness that existed in the Trinity. They were also able to experience something of the ecstasy of that union. In fulfilling God's command in this garden of delights, they would experience the delights of each other (see Song of Songs 4:12–5:1). Finally, they were able to share in the divine love that spilled over from their love for each other into the act of creation. They would feel what God felt when He first cradled them in His arms, looking into their faces, and seeing something of His face (see Gen. 5:3). It was such an overwhelming feeling that He just had to share the experience with them.

God's love was also in their assignment to rule. God wanted them to know Him—to know what His work was like and how He went about doing it. He ruled not as a bullying tyrant but as a benevolent monarch. He didn't coerce; He coaxed. His yoke was easy; His burden was light. God knew that if men were to be rulers, whether exercising dominion over children, over tribes, or over nations, the best way for them to learn that was to become ranchers, ruling over livestock. In the process of dealing with animals that were thirsty, weary, wounded, stubborn, or lost, they would learn something about how God exercises His dominion. Whether He leads us into green pastures, beside still waters, or through the valley of the shadow of death, all His guidance in our lives comes from love. Whether He is protecting us with His rod or prodding us with His staff, all His intervention in our lives comes from love.

Finally, God's love was behind their mission to tend the garden. Peter Kreeft, in his book *The God Who Loves You,* summarizes it this way:

> The point of the command to tend the garden (earth) is that God wants us to learn to love Him through loving other people and to learn to love other people through loving subhuman things. It starts at the lowest level with vegetables and fruits, then animals, then humans, and then God. Love is not jealous. God wants to share with us as much of Himself and His love with us as possible, including His love for the earth.[1]

LOVE IN THE PROHIBITION

It is easier to see the love of God in what He gives us than in what He withholds from us. But if you look with the right eyes, you can see it. Here is the prohibition:

And the LORD God commanded the man, saying, "Of every tree of the garden you may freely eat; but of the tree of the knowledge of good and evil you shall not eat, for in the day that you eat of it you shall surely die" (Genesis 2:16-17).

This prohibition raises some important questions. What *was* the tree? And why was it forbidden?

To answer those questions, let's look how the phrase, "the knowledge of good and evil," is used elsewhere in the Scriptures. Two passages in particular are illuminating.

Moreover your little ones and your children, who you say will be victims, who today have no knowledge of good and evil, they shall go in there; to them I will give it, and they shall possess it (Deuteronomy 1:39).

Here the reference is to little children who are too young to realize the difference between right and wrong. Children explore the world around them innocently, full of curiosity, trust, and wonder, until they come to a boundary bordering on territory that is potentially dangerous. That is when a parent steps in and helps them learn to discern what is good for them and what is not. "Eat your vegetables," a parent may say one moment. And the next moment that same parent may say, "Don't eat your crayons."

Judging the difference between what is good for them and what is harmful is an essential skill for children to learn if they are to grow up healthy. Judging the shortcomings of another person is not. Judging the sin of another person is not. Judging, in fact, is contrary to love. For love covers sin rather than exposes it (see 1 Pet. 4:8). The consensus of the New Testament is that if we judge, we don't love; and if we love, we don't judge.

Wanting to sit in the seat of judgment is wanting to sit on the very throne of God. At least Joseph thought so. Listen to his words to the brothers who, years before, had belittled him, betrayed him, and left him for dead. Now Joseph is in Egypt, sitting in a place of authority, and his brothers come to him, impoverished, begging not just for food but for forgiveness.

> *Then his brothers also went and fell down before his face, and they said, "Behold, we are your servants." Joseph said to them, "Do not be afraid, for am I in the place of God? But as for you, you meant evil against me; but God meant it for good, in order to bring it about as it is this day, to save many people alive. Now therefore, do not be afraid; I will provide for you and your little ones." And he comforted them and spoke kindly to them* (Genesis 50:18-21).

Joseph knew the difference between what was good and what was evil, but he didn't use that knowledge to elevate himself to a place of judgment. He felt *that* place should be reserved only for God. To him, judgment was a divine boundary that no human should cross. To do so was tantamount to trespassing.

In his book, *Repenting of Religion,* Gregory Boyd explains why:

When we judge others negatively, we stand in the place of God. We leave the proper domain given to us, with its vocational description to be God-like in how we love, and we move to the center to carry out a job that belongs only to the One who rightly occupies the center. We eat of the fruit of the Tree of the Knowledge of Good and Evil and thus do not love.

Jesus commands us not to violate the prohibition at the center of life. Surrendering all judgment to God, we are to look past people's sins. We are to believe and hope for the best in others (1 Cor. 13:7). In fact, when the sin is against us, our focus should be on how God can creatively use this offense to further His good purposes for our lives, just as Joseph did.[2]

The prophet Isaiah looks back on the torturous path of history since the Fall, and he traces it back to satan, who had trespassed the same boundary that Adam and Eve were about to trespass.

> *How you are fallen from heaven, O Lucifer, son of the morning! How you are cut down to the ground, you who weakened the nations! For you have said in your heart: "I will ascend into heaven, I will exalt my throne above the stars of God; I will also sit on the mount of the congregation on the farthest sides of the north; I will ascend above the heights of the clouds, I will be like the Most High"* (Isaiah 14:12-14).

The love in prohibiting Adam and Eve from eating of the Tree of the Knowledge of Good and Evil was God's attempt to spare the first couple from making the same mistake that satan had made so they would not have to endure the disastrous consequences that would follow. God wanted them to be fully, joyfully, and eternally human, which meant that they were to get life from loving, not judging.

LOVE IN THE CONDEMNATION

Genesis 3:8-24 chronicles the consequences of disobedience. Following the fateful choice to eat from the forbidden tree, Adam and Eve experienced the first consequence. They got new eyes—but not Heaven's eyes. They got fallen eyes, eyes that were filled with fear and shame. Their first estrangement was from God. Whereas they used to love hearing the sound of God walking through the garden in the cool of the day, now they feared it. Whereas they used to walk freely and openly in the garden, now they hid self-consciously and shamefully. They covered themselves with fig leaves to hide their shame. And we have been covering ourselves with one thing or another ever since, hoping it will hide us.

> *Then the eyes of both of them were opened, and they knew that they were naked; and they sewed fig leaves together and made themselves coverings. And they heard the sound of the LORD God*

walking in the garden in the cool of the day, and Adam and his wife hid themselves from the presence of the LORD God among the trees of the garden. Then the LORD God called to Adam and said to him, "Where are you?" So he said, "I heard Your voice in the garden, and I was afraid because I was naked; and I hid myself" (Genesis 3:7-10).

Their second estrangement was from each other. Notice how Adam passes judgment. He directly blames his wife; then indirectly he blames God.

*And He said, "Who told you that you were naked? Have you eaten from the tree of which I commanded you that you should not eat?" Then the man said, "The **woman** whom **You** gave to be with me, she gave me of the tree, and I ate"* (Genesis 3:11-12).

It's Eve's turn to face God, and she, too, passes the blame: *"And the LORD God said to the woman, 'What is this you have done?' The woman said, 'The serpent deceived me, and I ate'"* (Gen. 3:13).

The testimony of the witnesses has been heard. The defense rests. Now it is time for the verdict to be rendered.

So the LORD God said to the serpent: "Because you have done this, you are cursed more than all cattle, and more than every beast of the field; on your belly you shall go, and you shall eat dust all the days of your life. And I will put enmity between you and the woman, and between your seed and her Seed; He shall bruise your head, and you shall bruise His heel" (Genesis 3:14-15).

The last part of the judgment is cryptic, but the ramifications are cosmic. War has broken out in the universe. The creation has rebelled against its Creator, choosing to ally itself with the archenemy of God. The picture is of a Coming One who will defeat the serpent with a victorious stamp of His foot, but not until the serpent first inflicts a venomous bite on His heel. The war that has broken out in Eden will one day be won by a Deliverer whom God will send through the offspring of the woman. That is where the love is—in the promise.

> *To the woman He said: "I will greatly multiply your sorrow and your conception; in pain you shall bring forth children; your desire shall be for your husband, and he shall rule over you"* (Genesis 3:16).

God hasn't discarded them, starting over with a new couple. He allows them to continue to represent Him by bearing His image, and to continue to rule by reproducing that image. The sentence of death will be stayed. That is where the love is. The couple will be able to live long enough so they can bear and raise children, and Adam acknowledges this when he names his wife in verse 20. She will be called Eve, the mother of all *the living*, not the mother of all *the dying*.

> *Then to Adam He said, "Because you have heeded the voice of your wife, and have eaten from the tree of which I commanded you, saying, 'You shall not eat of it': Cursed is the ground for your sake; in toil you shall eat of it all the days of your life. Both thorns and thistles it shall bring forth for you, and you shall eat the herb of the field. In the sweat of your face you shall eat bread till you return to the ground, for out of it you were taken; for dust you are, and to dust you shall return." And Adam called his wife's name Eve, because she was the mother of all living* (Genesis 3:17-20).

When the verdict was spoken, a chain of events was set in motion. The world—and everything in it—started to die. The curse infected everything from the smallest microbe to the largest mammal. All biological clocks started winding down. All ordered systems reversed themselves and started moving toward disorder. All life was reset to follow a cycle of birth, growth, death, and decay.

Once again, the judgment seems harsh, but if we look at it through Heaven's eyes we will see that love for the entire future of humanity was the motivating reason. Pride was the motivation of the couple wanting to be like God. The solution to keeping pride from running its tragic course was to fix within the creative order something that would humble the human heart. So God, in a redemptive measure to bring humanity back to Him, decreed that nature would resist man's dominance, wrestling with him every day until one day pinning him to the ground in a final defeat. No matter how high man exalted himself, nature would bring him low. In bringing him low, it would humble him. And in humbling him, it would make him receptive to grace.

Death is the ultimate humbling when the condemned one in us cries out, *"Remember me when You come into Your kingdom"* (Luke 23:42).

The dying grace that is extended to us is the same one extended to the thief on the cross: *"Assuredly, I say to you, today you will be with Me in Paradise"* (Luke 23:43).

LOVE IN THE EXPULSION

After the individual verdicts are rendered, the Trinity takes counsel together in their chambers. The deliberation is of utmost seriousness. For a fate worse than the Fall looms on the horizon.

> *Then the LORD God said, "Behold, the man has become like one of Us, to know good and evil. And now, lest he put out his hand and take also of the tree of life, and eat, and live forever"—therefore the LORD God sent him out of the garden of Eden to till the ground from which he was taken. So He drove out the man; and He placed cherubim at the east of the garden of Eden, and a flaming sword which turned every way, to guard the way to the tree of life* (Genesis 3:22-24).

Once again, the sentence seems harsh, but once again, we need Heaven's eyes to look beyond the harshness. The reason for the expulsion from Eden was not punitive but preventative. Look closely at the words, *"lest he put out his hand and take also of the tree of life, and eat, and live forever."*

Because of the previous verdict, Adam and Eve were trapped in dying bodies. Death is the only thing that could free them. But, if they ate from the tree of life, they would live forever. Forever in a body that was in a constant state of decay. You can imagine the horrors they would become. It would be a nightmare they could never wake up from.

Barring the gates of Paradise and placing the strongest of angels to guard it was the only loving thing that could be done.

Exile is a judgment that is made from time to time in the Scriptures. But behind the judgment is love. The nation of Israel had its time of exile, first to Assyria, then later to Babylonia. Each was a hard, but an ultimately redemptive time, just as poverty, famine, and a pigsty in the distant country were in the story of the Prodigal Son (see Luke 15:11-32). All were providentially arranged to bring the son to his senses and put him on a path that would lead him home to his father's heart. The purpose of the exile was to bring the nation back to God so that they too could experience the blessings of home.

Expulsion from home leads to a longing for home (see Ps. 137:1-6). And the longing for home leads hopefully to a return to home—not just for a prodigal nation or a prodigal son, but for the prodigal in all of us who at one time or another leaves home for a distant country with its forbidden fruit hanging on all the low branches and its juicy promises of happiness apart from God.

OUR HOMESICKNESS FOR EDEN

This longing for Eden seems universal. It appears in all cultures, in every time period. In Jean Delumeau's book, *History of Paradise: The Garden of Eden in Myth and Tradition,* the author notes that:

> Many civilizations believed in a primordial paradise that was characterized by perfection, freedom, peace, happiness, abundance, and the absence of duress, tensions, and conflicts. In that paradise human beings got on well together and lived in

harmony with the animals. They also communicated effortlessly with the divine world. This belief gave rise in the collective unconsciousness to a profound nostalgia for the lost but not forgotten paradise and to a strong desire to recover it.[3]

Secular writers, such as Plato, Homer, Virgil, Horace, and Ovid, all wrote about Paradise, referring to it by different names: the Golden Age, the Elysian Fields, the Happy Isles. Sacred writers, such as Justin Martyr, Tertullian, Clement of Alexandria, and St. Basil, all believed that the Greek and Roman myths were inspired by the Hebrew account of Eden.

Early mapmakers, many of whom worked in monasteries, placed Eden on the top of their maps, which is why East, not North, was the orientation of all maps. Belief in the existence of Eden launched countless expeditions with explorers looking for the lost Paradise that offered everything from untold riches to a fountain of youth. That belief even captured the imagination of Christopher Columbus. In 1498, in his report on his third voyage, where he reached the mouth of the Orinoco River in South America, he wrote,

> Holy Scripture testifies that our Lord made the earthly Paradise in which he placed the Tree of Life....
>
> I do not find and have never found in any Greek or Latin writings which definitely state the worldly situation of the earthly Paradise, nor have I seen any world map which establishes its position except by deduction....
>
> I believe that, if I pass below the Equator, on reaching these higher regions I shall find a much cooler climate and a greater difference in the stars and waters. Not that I believe it possible to sail to the extreme summit or that it is covered by water, or that it is even possible to go there. For I believe that the earthly Paradise lies here, which no one can enter except by God's leave....[4]

Even in the 16th and 17th centuries, during the Renaissance, when belief in an earthly Paradise waned, people still longed for it nostalgically. It was during this period of unbelief that accounts of a lost golden age flourished in literature. This, for example, is when Thomas More's *Utopia* was published (1516). Elaborate walled gardens also flourished, not only in monasteries but in royal estates. Often the garden had a fountain in the middle of it that watered the rest of the garden, just as in Eden.

I personally believe that not only is our DNA passed from generation to generation but also some kind of encoded recollections from the past. We all have a nostalgic ache for Eden, which is none other than a universal longing for Heaven. C.S. Lewis believed so. In his book, *The Problem of Pain,* he wrote,

> There have been times when I think we do not desire heaven
> but more often I find myself wondering whether, in our heart
> of hearts, we have ever desired anything else.[5]

I know that it is true of me. The longing for Eden draws me like the point on a compass to a magnet. Especially over the past many years as I have traveled to the far corners of the world, searching for beauty and some remnant, no matter how tattered, of Eden.

My search has taken me on 12 safaris. On my tenth one, my wife and I had just crested the ridge of mountain in Tanzania that brought us to the edge of the Ngorongoro Crater. The guide stopped the land cruiser. A panorama of paradise stretched before us. Flocks of flamingos wading in the shallow end of a lake, looking like a splash of pink across a broad, blue canvas. Herds of zebras, whose stripes stood out like ancient writing on an open scroll of brown papyrus. Thompson gazelles, leisurely eating grass, their heads suddenly rising and turning in our direction. A few bounded away like spring-operated toys. The rest returned to grazing. Other animals threaded their way casually through herds, unconcerned and unafraid.

The beauty was breathtaking. Tears filled my eyes, blurring the edges of this nostalgic glimpse of the kingdom that once was and the anticipatory glimpse of the Kingdom that was to come. The guide asked, "Is this your first time to see it?"

I shook my head. "No, it is my tenth." I never grow tired of seeing it. Each time I do, it sets my heart to longing. It makes me want to do everything I can to bring something of Heaven down to earth. That is why, wherever I go in my "east-of-Eden" travels, I try to bring something of the atmosphere of Eden with me, with all the life-giving waters of love, all the sweet scents of joy, and all soothing music of unity.

We saw other animals, too. The sight almost made me laugh and did make me wonder. What fun God must have had designing each animal—deciding whether to make the zebra white with black stripes or black with white stripes, and how to style its mane. I can almost hear the conversation among the three of Them—Mohawk or shag—what do you think? And the elephant, seriously. That vacuum-cleaner hose of a snout, snuffling about the floor for any morsel of food; that swishy duster of a tail—and both of them bookending that bloat of a body.

One of the most amazing sights we saw was a Thompson gazelle giving birth right next to our vehicle. I almost had to stop my wife from jumping out and helping the mother. Then I almost had to stop her again after the mother had given birth. The baby was so vulnerable, its legs so skinny and frail, trying so hard to figure out how to use them, how to raise itself on all fours.

Not long ago I saw the movie *The Bucket List,* which is a story about two terminally ill men who write a list of things they want to do before they "kick the bucket." It was an intriguing premise for a movie. After seeing it, I wondered what would be *my* "bucket list." I wanted to see everything beautiful that still remained on this earth, no matter where it was or how hard it was to get there.

A couple of years ago, I was on an airplane, and I picked up a magazine with the words, "Heaven on Earth," in bold print across the cover. I leafed through it until I came to the article and the most enchanting pictures that accompanied it. When I finished reading, I knew I had to go there. So, leaving Manila in the Philippines, I flew to Palavana. From there I took a boat to El Nido. I couldn't believe all I saw, all I felt. It was the closest to Paradise I have ever been. The beauty. The fragrance. The lush abundance of fruits and flowers. The love, the joy, the feeling of being one with the environment. And, as if I had eaten the healing fruit from the tree of life, it was the only time that I hadn't experienced chronic pain in my spine since April 2, 1995, when I suffered a life-altering accident.

Every time I travel through some beautiful part of the world, like the Ngorongoro Crater or El Nido, my heart aches with a longing so strong it almost hurts. In that ache, I realize that I was made for Eden, made to enjoy all the gifts that were there in such abundance—life, health, loving relationships, joyful work, peace, harmony, and, most of all, conversing with God as we walk together through the garden in the cool of the day.

Living east of Eden, it is easy to focus on the thorns that line the stem of the rose. But the rose is still there. It still blooms. It still ladles out its fragrance to a world longing for Eden. Beauty is everywhere, if only we have eyes to see. We can complain that roses come with thorns, or we can be grateful that thorns come with roses. It's all a matter of perspective. Sometimes it is hard to see beauty springing out of barrenness, but even in the ugliest parts of the world you can see vestiges of Eden all around.

I personally have seen beauty in the most unimaginable places, in people you would least expect to see it. I saw God's generosity, for example, in a refugee camp in Sudan. I saw God's smile in a prison in the Philippines. I spent the night with the street children of Kilimani, Mozambique, and I witnessed in them a genuine hunger for God and supernatural courage. I saw radical Muslim leaders eagerly learning about God's love. I saw the joy of the Lord in the persecuted church in the Middle East. I saw hope sparkling in the eyes of a quadriplegic, in the hearts of the blind, and on the faces of the deaf and the broken.

WHAT WENT WRONG?

Back to our original question—what could possibly go wrong in such an edenic setting as Adam and Eve enjoyed?

To know what went wrong we don't need to understand the nature of man, but the nature of God. Since the essence of God is love, everything He does comes from there. Every thought, every word, every action. Love was the reason He created the universe. Love was the reason He created the earth. Love was the reason He created humanity, from Adam and Eve to you and me.

When God created us, He could have made us to love Him. He could have programmed us to obey His every command. He could have hard-wired us to pray to Him, including the very words of our prayers—all the way from "if it be Thy will" to "in Jesus' name." He could have written a software program that would automatically have us "give thanks in all things." He could have programmed a default that would immediately have us "consider it all joy" when we encountered various trials. He could have even queued His favorite praise music in us, and, by some feat of animatronics, coordinated our mouths to move in sync with it, all the way to the raising of our hands and the shedding of our tears.

God could have made what to us would seem the perfect human being, without the capacity to question, to doubt, to sin, to rebel. If He had, though, there would be one problem. We would also be without the capacity to love, because love, by its very nature, is a decision by a will that is free to choose—to love or not to love.

Love, if it is *truly* love, must be freely chosen, without compulsion or coercion. If it were otherwise, we would not be human but rather human*oid*—an elaborately designed computer system, resembling the image of God, housed in a life-like body, covered with simulated skin, connected to electrodes that fed information into a state-of-the-art CPU.

But *that* scenario would have been impossible.

Why?

Because it would go against the very nature of God. The Scriptures tell us that God cannot lie, because lying would go against His nature. In the same way, God can only act from love, because to do otherwise would go against the most fundamental part of His nature. To force us to love Him would be an act of fear, not of love—God would have to fear the possible consequences of creating a being that might rebel against Him, and that would be an act of paranoia.

So, if God wanted to create a universe that reflected His love, it involved a risk. A *huge* risk that would end up costing the Triune God a sum that is impossible for us, as humans, to calculate. It would cost the humiliation and death of one of Them—and They knew this when They counseled together to make man in Their image. That is what is so incredible. They knew the risk, and They went through with it anyway.

Somehow God felt *we* were worth the risk.

Which means He felt *I* was worth it.

And *you* were worth it.

Why?

That is the greatest mystery in the universe. Not *how* the universe came into existence. Not *when* the universe came into existence. But, given the risk, *why* the universe came into existence.

The answer is shrouded in mystery—the mystery of God's love. And no matter how powerful a telescope we make or how sophisticated a computer we design, we will never be able to fathom it.

All we can do is bow before the mystery.

THE READER'S PRAYER

Dear Father,

I bow before the mystery of Your love. Thank You! Thank You! Thank You!

Help me to realize who I am and who You are and never to confuse the two. Deliver me from my discontent, from my desire to have more, to control more. Give me a grateful heart for the abundance of gifts You have already given me, Lord.

Help me to see that judgment is one of those gifts, and that behind it, no matter how harsh, is Your love.

Your mercies are indeed new every morning, not just in Eden but in every day of my life. Thank You for the longing for home that You have placed in my heart.

Help me to see that all my longings are leading me to the safety, security, and comfort of Your arms. May I settle for nothing less.

Thank You for the place that has been prepared for me in Heaven, and for all the unfulfilled dreams and desires here on earth, reminding me that this is not my home.

Sometimes I forget, Lord.

Thank You for every thorn and thistle, for every pain, every drop of sweat, that points me to a Paradise yet to come.

CHAPTER 6

SEEING OURSELVES AS BELOVED SONS AND DAUGHTERS

But when the time arrived that was set by God the Father, God sent His Son, born among us of a woman, born under the conditions of the law so that He might redeem those of us who have been kidnapped by the law. Thus we have been set free to experience our rightful heritage. You can tell for sure that you are now fully adopted as His own children because God sent the Spirit of His Son into our lives crying out, "Papa! Father!" Doesn't that privilege of intimate conversation with God make it plain that you are not a slave, but a child? And if you are a child, you're also an heir, with complete access to the inheritance (Galatians 4:4-7 MSG).

LIVING IN FORGETFULNESS

After the Fall, everything changed—with one exception. Nothing changed in terms of the place that Adam and Eve had in God's heart. Though their performance fell abysmally short, their position remained absolutely secure.

To demonstrate this, I want to turn your attention to the genealogy of Christ in Luke. When you read through the entire thing, the rhythms in the repetition almost seem like the refrains of a song. "Jesus is the son of Joseph," it starts. And so it goes, stanza after stanza, down through the generations, back to the beginning:

> *...Shem, the son of Noah, the son of Lamech, the son of Methuselah, the son of Enoch, the son of Jared, the son of Mahalalel, the son of Cainan, the son of Enosh, the son of Seth, the son of...* (Luke 3:36-38).

And then the crescendo..."*Adam, the son of God.*"

What a note to end on!

After the Fall, God didn't become a landowner and Adam a sharecropper. God was *still* a Father. Adam was *still* a son, and Eve was *still* a daughter. Their sin didn't change that. Neither did the sin of the prodigal son. He felt unworthy to be one, but he *was* one. His sin disgraced him but didn't disinherit him. And *our* sin—no matter how serious or how shameful—won't disinherit us, either.

It is our *position* in the family—not our *performance* in the family— that establishes our identity and entitles us to our inheritance. We can never be downgraded, disowned, or disinherited. We can't be written out of the Father's will. As His children, we are His heirs. As heirs, we have an inheritance, not just in the hereafter but in the here and now. Jesus says that everything the Father has is ours (see Luke 15:31). *Present tense.* And Paul says that we have "complete access" to it (see Gal. 4:7).

Although the identity of Adam and Eve as God's children was secure, the memory of their identity was not. Now and then, they forgot who they truly were. Here and there, they forgot how much they were truly loved. Little by little, they wandered farther from their true home. But though they lost their home, they never lost their longing for it. That was the legacy of the Fall. Now and then, we forget who we truly are, you and I. Here and there, we forget how much we are truly loved. Little by little, we wander farther from our true home. Peter Kreeft describes that legacy this way:

> What is home? What are we longing for? Not just our lost youth, but humanity's. Our individual past is a symbol of our racial past, not vice versa. We long not for 1955 or 1255 but for Eden, where we lost not just our youth but our identity. Who are we now? We're not sure; we all have amnesia. We feel like dethroned princes turned into frogs by a magic spell and awaiting another magic spell, the transforming kiss, to restore our true identity.[1]

The familiar fairy tale of the frog-prince is merely an imaginative re-telling of the Gospel. The fairy tale teaches us that we must be loved in all our ugliness before we can become beautiful, which is merely another way of saying that while we were yet sinners, Christ died for us (see Rom. 5:8). Here is the point, both of the fairy tale and of the Gospel. It doesn't matter how loathsome the frog is. It doesn't matter how slimy his skin, or how warty; how disgusting his diet, or how repulsive his tongue; how bloated his belly, or how bugged-out his eyes. It doesn't matter what *the frog* is. All that matters is what *God* is. He is, above all, a Lover. And as a Lover, He sees with different eyes. He sees the prince we can become—or the princess—and humbles Himself, even disgraces Himself, to coronate us with His kiss.

With that kiss, we remember who we are.

And how much we are loved.

Living From Drudgery

When I looked back over the sheet music of my spiritual life, I saw notes of grace everywhere—quarter-notes, half-notes, full-notes. The notes came together to form lines, which in turn came together to form themes. The themes rose and fell in movements of joy and sorrow, faith and doubt, hope and despair.

One movement led to another, one stanza to another, and it all bore traces of God's hand, as if He were composing it. Still, something seemed missing. I practiced constantly, hitting the notes on the page and hitting them perfectly, but I wasn't making music—at least, not music that those around me much wanted to dance to. I felt Jesus' frustration when He told off the Pharisees with the indictment that He had played the flute for them, but they didn't dance. I wasn't sure what was wrong. All I knew was that it wasn't fun anymore—preaching, teaching, counseling, witnessing, personal Bible study, prayer—none of it was fun anymore.

In another of his books, *Seeing Is Believing,* Gregory Boyd sums up where I was:

> The more we experience the truth of who God is and the truth of who we are in Christ, the more our experienced self-identity becomes restored to the beautiful God-dependent relationship for which we were originally created. Our need for love and worth is increasingly met as we grow in our dependency upon the one who alone can meet it. We become human *beings* instead of human *doings,* for our worth is established in *who we are* rather than in *what we do.* As we experience the inherent love God has toward us and the worth God gives to us, we increasingly come to reflect this love and worth in our own identities.[2]

Like Adam and Eve, I had become a human *doing* instead of a human *being.* And like them, I had believed a lie about God and a lie about myself. I believed that *I* wasn't enough, that I needed to *be* more. And to be more, I believed that I needed to *do* more. You see, I felt my worth was determined by my performance. Consequently, I saw God's blessings not as wealth I had inherited but as wages I had worked for. Because of that, I never felt any job security. I lived from paycheck to paycheck, not as an honored partner, sharing in the family business...but as an hourly employee, punching the clock.

If I failed in my performance, I felt shameful. If I excelled in my performance, I felt prideful. Either way, my worth was determined by me, not by God. To make sure I performed well, I practiced long and hard. I could play by rote, it was all so familiar to me now. I knew which prayers to pray, and for how long. I knew which Bible verses to quote, and why. I knew what questions to ask, and when to ask them.

I had it all down pat, yet something was missing. It didn't make any difference how hard I tried. It wasn't good enough. And I could only conclude that it wasn't good enough because *I* wasn't good enough. I wasn't working hard enough, wasn't working long enough, or seriously enough. In my system of values, my worth was determined by my work. If I *worked* less, I felt *worth* less. And I was feeling worthless more and more.

In music, there is something called a "home" line, which is the melody. Musical lines harmonize with the melody by leaving the home line and later returning. The melodic line is essential because all the harmonic lines get their cues from it. Maybe that's what was missing from my life—a melody. Maybe that is why my longing for home, for Eden, had been such a recurring theme in my life.

I'm going to trace the music of my life back to the beginning to give you a sense of the lineage of grace, but also to give you a sense of what was missing from my life. I will begin at the beginning and take you to the present day.

January 13, 1966. I was born in Norway to Norwegian parents, with a Norwegian accent. (OK, the accent came later.) I came into the world more with a whimper than with a bang, more like a few slight notes from a piccolo than one resounding beat on a bass drum.

July 4, 1975. I moved from the city where I had been born, moved from the security of the only home I had known, the only neighborhood, the only school, the only church. Suddenly I was the outsider, the new kid, the one with the accent. During this time I remember a missionary showing slides in our church, and I felt a distinct tug on my soul. It was as if God were giving me a glimpse of my future. It wasn't music yet, but it felt as if it were a protracted note on its way to becoming a musical line.

1978. I suffered a painful and humiliating experience of abuse, something I felt too ashamed to share with anyone. For years I kept it a secret. It lived in me like the most dissonant of noises, and I couldn't imagine anything beautiful ever coming from it.

1979. I came to Christ. It was a beautiful moment, followed by a succession of ugly ones. Shortly after coming to Christ, I went to youth group, where I experienced constant ridicule, which eventually led to me leaving home and living out a prodigal period in my life. It was a confused movement in the symphony, so to speak, filled with deep and sorrowful tones. During that time I lived in the shadows of drugs, sex, and alcohol until 1984, when I finally came home to my family and to the Lord.

1985. I experienced the baptism of the Holy Spirit. I also experienced a lightness in my own spirit, and a stirring in my spirit that I can only describe as a rising drum roll, something like a timpani. I knew the music was taking me some place, I just didn't know *where*. It happened in Waterford, Ireland, in a Catholic church. One day after mass, without anyone touching me, I ended up on the floor, overwhelmed by the Holy Spirit. I received power from Him, but I still had an orphan spirit. And I was still trying to get worth out of my performance.

1988. I met Jennifer, the woman who would later become my wife, and the music became lighter, more lovely. But when I entered college that same year, the music became more dull, like a drone.

March 25, 1989. We got married. I also entered seminary. Very serious movements in my life. A lot of joy, but I felt I needed to step up to the seriousness of my responsibilities.

1991. We moved back to Norway, where I helped run my father's business. The change was good, and hopeful. I also became senior pastor of Sandnes Baptist Church in Norway. I was young, full of zeal, and eager to play the music I had studied so long in seminary. As it turned out, the music didn't sound quite like it did in the textbooks.

1995. It was June, if I remember correctly. Randy Clark was visiting a church in Norway, and I was standing in line, waiting to be ministered to. Randy looked at me, laid hands on me, and told me that I was a bulldozer, that I was going to plow through the nations, and that people were going to follow me. Something inside me resonated with his word. It was as if music had been playing all my life, and it had finally found the lyrics.

It all seemed so wonderful. And then, it all took such a horrible turn. I was sitting in a hot tub with several other pastors, and one of them jumped from above the pool, landing on my neck. I was taken to the hospital and treated for a compression fracture. I couldn't preach, couldn't play catch with my son, and went on full sick leave. Chronic pain shattered my world. Each day was a struggle to get through. Headaches. Dizziness. Vertigo. I had to take drugs for the pain, drugs to help me sleep, and before long, I felt like a zombie. I didn't understand it. I thought I was going to be a bulldozer, not the one bulldozed. What in the world had gone wrong? I hadn't expected my life to be a pop song, but I didn't expect it to be a funeral dirge, either.

1998. I had a breakthrough when I went 40 days without pain. I felt like a new man. I flew to Europe with a revived sense of passion and mission, only to have it all end tragically on August 2nd.

August 2, 1998. I was a passenger in a sports car, and the driver lost control, smashing into a wall. The impact broke my back, broke my leg in several places, and I spent the next year having several surgeries, imprisoned in a body cast, shuttled in and out of various hospitals. It was like cymbals falling out of hands and crashing to the ground.

1999. I started Global Mission Awareness, a ministry to the nations. After the cacophony of the last year, this was one clear note that came out of it all. And it was a hopeful note that gets clearer and more beautiful with each passing day.

2000. I was in constant pain, still traveling, still preaching, still healing the sick. I was taking so much medication to get me through each day, to get me through each plane flight, each engagement, and back again. I truly don't know how I did it. I only know that I paid a price to do it. Then came a musical rest in my life that forever changed my life. It happened in Melbourne, Florida, at a Holiday Inn, where about a hundred people met for a "father/son" meeting. I had been experiencing severe depression for some time now. For most of my life, I had been a high achiever. My whole identity was based on performance. Increasingly, I felt as if I couldn't perform as well, and, I reasoned, if I couldn't perform as well, I couldn't be worth as much.

We were all sitting together in this large room, where Dennis Jernigan had been singing and playing the piano. He looked at me and said: "You're not an orphan, Leif. So don't think like one." I had constantly compared myself to others, and though I felt successful in their eyes, I didn't feel successful in God's. He seemed so far. I didn't cry, but I did curl into a fetal position. People gathered around me, laying hands on me, praying silently as Dennis started to play.

He played, "Daddy's Song," and I just lay there on the floor. All of a sudden, some of the insecurities of the nine-year-old I once was came back to me. Some of the abuses of the 12-year-old I once was came back to me. Some of the prodigal ways of the 13 to 18-year-old I once was came back to me. It was as if liquid love had been poured over me. Wave after wave of it flowed over me. This went on for hours. And I heard the Father say, "You are *Mine*. You are My *beloved*. You are My beloved *son*. I love you. I am well-pleased with you."

That is when I started to cry. And when I started, I couldn't stop.

God visited the adult in me, speaking to me about how I related to my wife, my kids. "If you're not comfortable with love," He told me, "you can't be comfortable with Me, because I *am* love."

The Father's love was what was missing from my life. It was the melodic line that all the other lines in my life were longing for. It was where everything converged, where everything harmonized, where everything came home.

2002. The changes continued to come to me with these wonderful Father-to-son talks, and He healed me of an orphan spirit. Later that year, while in Cuba, I was infected by parasites. During that time, God changed my ministry and my message. My ministry changed from signs and wonders to Father and family, from living as an orphan to living as a son, from doing to being.

2005. With increased demands on me, I traveled more and more, doing more and more, giving more and more, until I just couldn't take it anymore. I crashed. And from December 2 to December 30, I entered a treatment facility in California. I had been on strong medications for five years and had abused them for the past two. My body refused to take it anymore. For five months, I experienced the darkest period in my life. The Holy Spirit left me, and demonic spirits tormented me. My spiritual father, Jack Taylor, and his wife Frieda were there praying, keeping vigil, loving me through it all. At the end of it, I experienced a resurrection. But to get there I had to experience a death and burial. I died, a servant; I arose, a son. I no longer wanted to be a senior pastor, a senior leader, a senior spokesman, a senior *anything.* I just wanted to be a little boy with a big Papa.

November/December of 2008. For some unexplained reason, I suddenly started losing weight. I traveled all over the world during this time, wheezing when I breathed, having to stop when I carried my luggage, or climbed stairs. I came down with a 102 degree fever, hives, shingles, and then an even higher fever. I boarded a plane for home, and, when I arrived there, crashed. It was the night before Christmas. The hospital tests revealed double pneumonia. They also did a scan on my abdomen and found a major tumor, which they removed. Originally, it was thought to be parasitic in origin, but later it was discovered to be benign.

February 1, 2009. I had lost 46 pounds. Eight days before surgery to remove the tumor, I felt so miserable that I thought I was going to die.

My assistant, Leanne, sent out an email to our ministry partners. People all over the world prayed. One of my closest friends, Randy Clark, phoned me and said "Leif, we're praying and standing with you. If the enemy takes one of us out, he'll have to take all of us out, because we're family." Miraculously, I started feeling hopeful. After the surgery, my spiritual father, Jack Taylor, and I were meeting with a friend of his who's a surgeon. I had to lean forward to talk. The staples in my stomach hurt so much that I couldn't talk for very long, and I had to lean back in order to rest. Jack could feel something different in me. When I leaned backward, in rest, the Holy Spirit came upon me. And when I leaned forward, in release, the Holy Spirit went out through me. It was like the rhythms of Heaven that I talked about earlier—the rhythms of the waltz. Lean back, lean forward. Receive, release. It was as if God were teaching me something essential for the next movement of my life, but He had to put me on my back to do it.

The Present. As I place the sheet music of my life on a music stand and step back from it, I can see the rising and falling of the notes, the coming together of the musical lines, the emergence of its themes, and, over it all and through it all...the movements of grace. The biggest movement of grace was going from being a servant to being a son and living off the wealth of my inheritance rather than off the wages of my performance.

LIVING FROM DELIGHT

My journey from a beleaguered servant to a beloved son can be illustrated from the film, *Mr. Holland's Opus*.[3] It's a wonderful movie, and, if you haven't seen it, here is the story line. Mr. Holland, played by Richard Dreyfuss, is an aspiring composer as the story begins, hoping someday to create a great *opus*, which is the Latin word for "work." But he is married and has a child and must attend to other work—to the practical matter of providing for a family. So he gets a job as a high school music teacher, and for the duration of his career, his dreams of being a great American composer go begging.

When he retires from teaching, the school hosts a surprise assembly in his honor. On stage are his students, sitting with instruments in hand, waiting for him to conduct the work that for years he had labored in obscurity to create. It is then we realize—and perhaps he realizes, too—that the great American symphony he would be remembered for was not the one on their music stand, but the one he had written in their lives.

One of those students—now governor of the state—is a woman he once had in class. Earlier in the movie we see him struggling to help the tall, red-headed student learn to play the clarinet. Three scenes chart the progression of that subplot.

The first scene is the first day of band class, where Mr. Holland is trying to get a feel for the skills of his students. As the students play, it sounds as if they are torturing their instruments, and we get the feeling it's going to be a long year for the fledgling teacher.

As he listens, Mr. Holland spots a girl who is failing at the clarinet, a fact not only noticed by him but by everyone. He waves his baton for the students to stop.

"OK. OK. That wasn't bad. That wasn't bad at all." He looks over his glasses at the gangly girl slumping in her seat. "Ah…Ms.? …I'm sorry," he points to her, apologizing for not knowing her name.

"Lang," she says sheepishly.

"Pardon me?"

"Lang. Gertrude Lang."

"OK, Ms. Lang. Would you take it from bar 37?"

She puts her mouth on the reed of the clarinet and starts to play. The notes are painful to listen to, and the boys behind her catch each other's eyes, trying to hide their reaction.

"OK. OK. Good. Good." The bell rings. "Eh, that's enough for today. I'll see you all tomorrow. Very good work." As the students filter out of class, Mr. Holland says, "Ms. Lang, would you mind hanging for a moment please?"

Her countenance falls. She walks to the front of the room, her shoulders slumped, dreading the anticipated criticism.

"You seem to be having a little trouble getting through the break," he says.

Her face is without expression; her words, without life. "I know."

"How long have you been playing?"

"Three years," she says matter-of-factly.

He is taken aback. "*Really?*" He pauses, searching for words that won't crush her. "And do you find you get all the practice time that you need?"

"I practice constantly."

Mr. Holland pauses, then exhales, again searching for what to say. One well-meaning but ill-chosen word could devastate her. "Well. Then I think…I think maybe…you and I should find some time to work on an *individual* basis."

His words infuse her with life. You can see it in her eyes, hear it in her voice. "That would really be great."

"I don't have a lot of time—"

"That's OK. Whatever time you can give me, it doesn't matter." And by now, she is animated. "I *really, really, really* want to do good at this."

"I bet you do," he responds, suddenly wondering what he has gotten himself into. "Well, why don't you come in a half hour before first period tomorrow, and we'll just start…and—"

She is beside herself, beaming. "OK. Thank you." And she curtsies almost as a reflex. "Thank you very much."

He has made her day, and possibly he has saved a part of her from dying. That ends the first of three scenes of this subplot between teacher and student.

A number of scenes intervene, and then we come back to her. Only *this* time, the mood has changed. It is after school, and she is practicing alone in a small room. The music is like fingernails scraping across a blackboard. Her eyes are brimming with tears, and she is doing everything she can to keep them from bursting their banks.

Mr. Holland is leaving for the day, and on his way out he calls to her. "Give it up, Ms. Lang." As he walks away, he hears her crying. He stops and pauses, wondering what to tell her. Coming into the doorway, he explains, "School's out, Ms. Lang. I meant, give it up *for the day*."

She sniffs in her emotions. "I *know* what you meant."

"Then why are you crying?"

"I'm terrible," she says, the tears coming stronger now. "I'm terrible. I...I tried, and I just—"

And they are talking over each other now. "Ms. Lang.... it's a lot of work to learn a musical instrument—"

"I just want to be good at something." And a lifetime of pain spills out. She sits straight in her hard, wooden chair, gathering her emotions. "My sister got a ballet scholarship to Julliard. And my brother's going to Notre Dame on a football scholarship. My mother's won the blue ribbon for watercolor so many times they retired the category. And my father's got the most beautiful voice." The next words are so painful to dredge up that she almost can't do it. "I'm the only one in my family who...I, I, I just can't...it doesn't make any difference...anyway...I—" She can't go on. Getting up, she walks out.

At a loss for words, Mr. Holland can only stand there.

When she based her worth on performance and weighed her performance against the performances of others in her family, the scales always tipped in their favor. She felt worth less because her performance was less.

The next scene we see the young woman coming into the music room, where Mr. Holland is playing the piano softly to himself. She is poised, resolute, her long red hair parted in the middle and flowing down her shoulders.

"Mr. Holland?"

"You're late. And you left your clarinet here the other day."

"Yeah, I…If you know anybody who wants it—" He stops and turns. "I'm giving up the clarinet." A pause, as if she has rehearsed this. "I'm just goofing up everybody else anyway. I just wanted to say thanks, thanks for trying." She turns and walks to the door.

"Is it any fun?" His words stop her.

She turns, pausing a moment. "I wanted it to be."

Mr. Holland gets up from the piano bench with a sigh. "You know what we've been doing wrong, Ms. Lang? We've been playing the notes on the page." He puts a record on a nearby phonograph.

"Well, what else is there to play?"

"Well, there's a lot more to music than playing the notes on the page." The needle makes contact with the vinyl. The song is "Louie, Louie" by the Kingsmen. "These guys, for example. Now, they can't sing. And they have absolutely no harmonics. And they're playing the same three chords over and over again." He pauses. "And I *love* it." A smile comes to his face and the beginning of a laugh. "Do *you*?"

She smiles. "Yeah."

"Why?"

And we see life returning to her face. "I don't know."

"Yeah, you do."

She answers sheepishly, "Because it's fun?"

"That's right!" His passion builds. "Because playing music is supposed to be *fun*. It's about *heart*. It's about *feeling* and moving people and something beautiful and being alive, and it's *not* about the notes on a page. I can teach you the notes on a page. I *can't* teach you that other stuff." Again he pauses, thinking on his feet. "Do me a favor." He stops the phonograph. "Pick up your clarinet…and play *with* me." She picks up her instrument and sits in the chair. "This time," he says, as he takes away her music stand, "no music."

For a second she resists. "Oh."

"Because you *already* know it. It's already in your head and your fingers and your heart. You just don't trust yourself to know that." He takes his place at the piano next to her. "OK. Here we go. Ready? One, two, three, four."

The clarinet instrumental is Acker Bilk's signature song, "Stranger on the Shore." She follows him, but after a few seconds a squeaky note escapes. "Ah," she grimaces.

"OK. Do it again. This time, not so much lip on the mouthpiece. One, two, three, four."

But she does it again, this time scolding herself. "Oh!"

"No," he says. "Now don't *do* that."

He pauses. "Let me ask you a question. When you look at yourself in the mirror, what do you like best about yourself?"

Her eyes fall onto the long, red hair, cascading down her shoulders. "My hair."

He smiles, nodding, as if to agree. "Why?"

"My father always says it reminds him of the sunset."

This pleases him. He pauses, then says, "Play the sunset." Another pause, and he walks her through it. "Close your eyes." And she closes them. "One, two, three, four."

She follows his accompaniment, surprising herself at how easy it is, how *good* she is, how beautiful the music is that's coming from her instrument. She almost stops in amazement. Mr. Holland smiles, then laughs. *"Don't* stop playing!"

As she continues playing, he stops to watch her, marveling at the transformation taking place before his eyes. How do we explain the miracle that took place in that moment? When the young woman realized she wasn't auditioning for a part in the family—that she already *had* a place in the family, a secure place where she was unconditionally loved and unimaginably cherished—she could relax. No one in the family was judging her performance. And no one—least of all, her father—based her *worth* on her performance. Ironically, when there is no pressure to perform, it is amazing how that affects our performance. Pressure gives way to passion; fear, to love; drudgery, to fun.

GETTING PERSONAL

Let me ask you a question.

Is it any fun?

The Christian life you're living, the Christian God you're serving, the Christian things you're doing. *Is it any fun?* By fun, I don't mean that you're in a perpetual state of euphoria. I don't mean that you're always up, always in a good mood, always the life of the party. What I mean by the question is this. Do you love it? Is it your passion? Do you get joy from it? Does it give you life? And does it give life to those around you?

The Christian life is not about living up to the law; it's about living out of love. A passionate, all-consuming love. You shall love the Lord your God with all your...*what?* With all your heart. Life with the Father is about *heart.* It's about *feeling* and moving people and something beautiful and being alive, and it's *not* about the notes on a page. I can teach you the notes on a page. I *can't* teach you that other stuff. I can teach you how to study the Bible, how to pray, the importance of going to church, tithing, serving. But the Christian life is not an *education*; it's an *encounter*.

In Eugene Peterson's paraphrase of the Bible, called The Message, he chronicles Jesus' path to service, which begins with an encounter with the Holy Spirit and His heavenly Father.

> *The moment Jesus came up out of the baptismal waters, the skies opened up and He saw God's Spirit—it looked like a dove— descending and landing on Him. And along with the Spirit, a voice: "This is My Son, chosen and marked by My love, delight of My life"* (Matthew 3:16-17).

After Jesus was anointed by the Spirit, He was affirmed by the Father (see Matt. 3:16-17). After He was affirmed by the Father, He was tested by the devil (see Matt. 4:1-11). And after He was approved from His test, He was assigned to His task (see Matt. 4:12-25).

Knowing who He was and how much He was loved made all the difference in how Jesus went about His task. And it will make all the difference in how *you* go about *yours*. From that place of connection with the love in His Father's heart—from that place where His identity and worth were not only stored but treasured—He played the most enchanting music the world has ever heard. For those trained to believe that the notes on the page were all that mattered, it wasn't music they cared to dance to. But for others, the music was so beguiling, they left their homes, their jobs, everything, to join in the dance.

I wish I could teach you how to do that. But there are things that only the Holy Spirit can impart—like the Father's love. Believing in the Father's love is one thing; being baptized in it is another. That is why I use the phrase, *"Baptism* of Love." Because it's not an *indoctrination*; it's an *immersion*. The Holy Spirit immerses us in the Father's love. He does this by placing us on the Father's lap, so to speak, where the Father lovingly embraces us, pressing us against His chest so closely we can hear the music of His heart. Every swooshing beat of it. He presses us close so that *our* heart connects with *His*. And He keeps us close until the beat of His heart resets the beat of ours.

Once we have experienced *that*, we begin to love Him with *all* our heart, *all* our soul, *all* our strength. And everything changes. Everything within us—every thought, every feeling, every word, every action—beats in rhythm with His love.

Then we will no longer be playing the notes on the page.

We will be playing the sunset.

Though it may not set the whole world singing, here and there it may start some of the world humming. Now and then, even swaying. And little by little, dancing. Step by joyful step. Until, at last, lost in the revelry, we look up and realize…we have danced our way home!

THE READER'S PRAYER

Dear Papa,

I believe I am not a servant but a son or a daughter.

I believe it is not my performance that defines me but my position.

I believe I am not impoverished but that I have an inheritance, reserved in my name in Heaven that can be accessed in Your name here on earth.

I believe the Christian life is not about the notes on the page, not about how diligently I practice them, or how perfectly I perform them.

I believe the Christian life is about playing the sunset.

I believe it is about You drawing me close and keeping me close.

I believe it is about connecting to Your heart, feeling Your delight over my life, and living from that delight.

These things I believe.

Help me in my unbelief.

PART 3

SEEING OTHERS THE WAY
THE FATHER SEES THEM

The loveless one is blind; he sees only the caterpillar, while the lover sees the butterfly…. God believes in our butterfly, hopes for our butterfly, loves us as butterflies. —Peter Kreeft[1]

CHAPTER 7

SEEING HUMANITY
THROUGH HEAVEN'S EYES

*Now there was a certain disciple at Damascus named Ananias;
and to him the Lord said in a vision, "Ananias." And he said,
"Here I am, Lord." So the Lord said to him, "Arise and go to the
street called Straight, and inquire at the house of Judas for one
called Saul of Tarsus, for behold, he is praying. And in a vision
he has seen a man named Ananias coming in and putting his
hand on him, so that he might receive his sight." Then Ananias
answered, "Lord, I have heard from many about this man, how
much harm he has done to Your saints in Jerusalem. And here he
has authority from the chief priests to bind all who call on Your
name." But the Lord said to him, "Go, for he is a chosen vessel of
Mine to bear My name before Gentiles, kings, and the children of
Israel"* (Acts 9:10-15).

I love Peter Kreeft's thought that it is the *loveless one* who sees only the
caterpillar in us—slow and cumbersome, earthbound and bother-
some; while the *lover* sees the butterfly—in all its beauty, all its flitting

iridescence, moving from flower to flower, all its lilting movements in flight, making poetry out of thin air.

That is the way God sees *us*, you and me and everyone who has ever inched his way on this earth. He sees not our history but our destiny. Not what we once were but what we will one day become. He sees not our drizzly gray past but our sun-washed future, a rainbow full of promise arching over the whole of it. For God sees not as man sees. We see the disgusting sinner; He sees the destined saint.

Take Saul, for instance. When God saw him, He saw him not as Ananias saw him—a radical, religious terrorist who was determined to stamp out Christianity—but as a chosen vessel to bear His name to the nations.

It wasn't the first time the eyes of Heaven looked upon our humanity and saw butterflies when everyone else saw caterpillars.

When everyone saw an old man and a barren woman, God saw a nation so great it would outnumber the stars in the heavens (Abraham and Sarah; see Gen. 15:15; 17:17). When everyone else saw a sheep-herder, God saw a giant-killer (David; see 1 Sam. 17:15,49). When everyone else saw a mere wheat thresher, God saw a mighty warrior (Gideon; see Judg. 6:11; 8:28). When everyone else saw a tender of sycamores and a gatherer of figs, God saw a deeply rooted, hard-barked, unswaying tree of a prophet (Amos; see Amos 7:14-15).

When Jesus came to earth, He brought His heavenly eyes with Him, seeing our humanity the way His Father did—seeing us as butterflies, believing in our butterfly, hoping for our butterfly, loving us as butterflies. When everyone else saw fishermen, He saw fishers of men (Peter, Andrew, James, and John in Matthew 4:18-22). When everyone else saw prodigals in pigsties, He saw sons and daughters gathered around His dining table (the sinners Jesus ate with in Luke 15:1-2). When everyone else saw a ranting, demon-possessed man, Jesus saw a clear-eyed, clear-headed evangelist (the Gerasene demoniac in Mark 5:1-20).

Wouldn't it be great to have that kind of perspective on people? Wouldn't it be great to see humanity through Heaven's eyes? To see the Sauls of the world not as the Church's greatest persecutors but as its greatest proponents. To see Muslims not as a problem but as a promise. To see not the ugliness of the caterpillar but the beauty of the butterfly that resides in it as a dormant miracle awaiting its emergence and its destined moment to fly and grace the world with its loveliness.

So. How does one go about getting eyes like that?

I'll tell you how I got mine. It was a process of transformation, not unlike how the caterpillar is transformed into a butterfly. To illustrate, I want to refer to Sue Monk Kidd's book on spiritual transformation, titled, *When the Heart Waits.* Here is how she describes the transformation that took place in *her* life:

> I was standing on the shifting ground of midlife, having
> come upon that time in life when one is summoned to an
> inner transformation, to a crossing over from one identity to
> another. When change-winds swirl through our lives, espe-
> cially in midlife, they often call us to undertake a new passage
> of the spiritual journey: that of confronting the lost and coun-
> terfeit places within us and releasing our deeper, innermost
> self—our *true* self. They call us to come home to ourselves, to
> become who we really are.[1]

She might as well have been talking about *me,* for it was in *my* midlife when the ground beneath *me* began to shift, when the winds of change were swirling all around *me.* Little did I realize that God was simply saying through the circumstances of my life, "It is time." It is time that Leif finds out his *real* identity, his *true* self. He was bringing me to a place where I had to confront the lost and counterfeit places within me. He was bringing me *home* so I could become who I *really* and *truly* am.

You see, the Gospel had brought me to the Cross, but the Cross had not brought me home. I came to Christ, but not to the Father. And so, even though I was a son, I felt like an orphan, and I lived like an orphan—anxious, distrustful, insecure. I had a safe and secure place in God's heart, but I was still on the street, so to speak: living day to day; alone and afraid; a soul in tatters, tired and footsore, desperately trying to find its way home.

I loved Jesus, my Brother, but I knew so very little of His Father, who was also *my* Father—it just didn't seem that way. He seemed distant and detached, at times, even unapproachable. I didn't know how to come close to Him. So *He* came close to *me*. And in doing so, He showed me my true identity.

It didn't happen overnight but over time. As you saw in the last chapter, the process of transformation is just that—a *process*. Not unlike the process whereby a caterpillar becomes a butterfly. There are three stages to that process: first, the larval stage; then, the cocoon stage; and finally, the butterfly stage.

My emergence from the cocoon happened that night with a group of people in Melbourne, Florida, when Dennis Jernigan spoke to me and sang to me as he played "Daddy's Song" on the piano. I was folded into a fetal position, and I felt as if I were in a cocoon of some sort. "You're not an orphan, Leif. Don't act like one," Dennis said. Those words split open my cocoon. And the *new* me, with wings still wet, emerged. When I got up from the floor, I felt the stretching of my wings, drying themselves, tentative yet eager to take flight.

The process of transformation is nothing short of a miracle, both in the natural realm and in the spiritual realm. Do you know how a caterpillar is transformed into a butterfly? Something mysterious begins to stir inside the caterpillar, prompting it to form a cocoon. Once inside the cocoon, the caterpillar is trapped. It can't leave. It can't move. It can't do anything. All it can do is lie there and wait—the way the body of Jesus, wrapped in those confining grave clothes, had to lie entombed in the darkness and wait—for its resurrection. And so must we, you and I, if we want to live in the newness of the resurrected life. We lie there in the dark, bound head to foot by confining circumstances. We lie there, not the one acting but the one acted upon. And there, in the darkness, we wait. And wait. And wait.

Until it is time. *Our* time. Our *appointed* time to emerge and reveal to the watching world the soaring beauty of what we were all created to be.

Before this emergence, though, something terrible happens; that is, if you believe your *true* identity is a caterpillar and you are determined to *stay* a caterpillar even if it kills you. God knows that this creature was not destined to spend the rest of its life worming around on the earth; it was destined to fly. But how do you convince a caterpillar of that, especially one that has grown comfortable *being* a caterpillar and is stubbornly wanting to *remain* a caterpillar? After all, he's pretty good at being a caterpillar. Added to that, all his friends are caterpillars. He's familiar with the ground, knows the lay of the land, and is comfortable with his place in the meadow.

What God does that seems so terrible is that He starts to dissolve the caterpillar. All the internal organs, all the external appendages, *everything* turns to liquid. Halfway through the process, the caterpillar is no longer a caterpillar; it is gooey mess. Out of this mess comes the miracle. Out of *most* messes comes the miracle. Both your messes and my messes. The miracle is this: out of this shapeless mass of goo God causes the cells to reorganize and build a butterfly, a being that is totally beyond the caterpillar's wildest imagination.

You can imagine—if that caterpillar had a sophisticated nerve network like we do—how it would feel to have your body slowly dissolve. It would feel like the Wicked Witch in *The Wizard of Oz* who was doused with water and started to shrink, screaming, "I'm melting! I'm melting!"

You can imagine, too, if the nerves were still active, what they must have thought there in the darkness as the caterpillar's shapelessness began to take shape. Its only thought, its only longing, its only prayer is to be restored to its original worminess. To crawl the earth again, on ground that didn't shift. To chew leaves again, on sturdy stalks that supported its weight. That's all. That's not too much to ask, is it?

One thing I found out about the Father's love. Though He loves us as we are, He loves us too much to let us *remain* as we are.

But what does a caterpillar know of such things? *Wings*. Who ever heard of such things, such far-fetched, fairy-tale kinds of things? *Flight*. How scary would *that* be, not having solid ground beneath you? *The nectar of flowers*. Who could ever want anything better to eat than the chewy greenness of leaves?

You can almost hear the conversation between the caterpillar and its Creator.

"No!" comes the scream from the liquid. "Don't give me wings; give me back my legs. Don't fill me with fantasies of flight; solid ground is good enough for me. And don't entice me with some fabled drink from flowered goblets; give me my greens and leave me be, to live in peace and to eat in peace."

That extended metaphor captures what had been happening to me. From the compressed vertebrae in the hot tub accident to the shattered bones in the car accident to the multiple surgeries to the constant and excruciating pain to the pain killers to the addiction to rehab. I couldn't understand where God was in all of this, why He allowed so much pain to come into my life. What I *couldn't* see then that I *can* see now is that I was in a cocoon, a dark and confining cocoon. For five months it was the darkest time in my life, the most confining time in my life, and the most confusing. What was happening to me? What in the world was happening to me?

I was melting.

And I was miserable.

I say all this to tell you that pain is part of the process of transformation. Perhaps it *is* the process. I would be a snake-oil salesman if I told you otherwise. I had much pain leading up to my emergence from the cocoon I had been in. I have much pain still. It is chronic and often acute. Having given up the painkillers, I have to live with the pain. Each day I have to live with it, getting reprieves measured in hours, not days. I trust that God is in the pain somehow—not only *with* me in the pain, but loving and transforming me through it.

So, here's the fine print in the vacation brochure that most travel agents don't tell you. To see other people through Heaven's eyes means you have to lose your earthly eyes. How do you do that? How did the caterpillar get the eyes of the butterfly? Through a process of *isolation*, *transformation*, and *emergence*. God sets you apart by cocooning you; then one day you emerge from the cocoon, and He releases you into the world—to fly!

In the terrifying middle of that process, though, He dissolves you. The old you, that is. The lost you. The orphan you. The anxious you. The you that believes your true identity is a caterpillar. The you that perhaps stubbornly wants to *remain* a caterpillar.

Here is what you need to understand. The process of transformation—getting new eyes with which to see, new wings with which to fly—is a painful one. But what emerges from the transformation is worth the pain. And what emerges is your truest self, your most beautiful self, the self that the world is needing to see, longing to see, aching to see.

I emerged from that process a lover. Not a preacher, not an evangelist, not a missionary. A lover—which is hard for some people to understand. For instance, the man I sat next to on an eight-hour plane trip.

We introduced ourselves. I asked him what he did, and he told me he was a senior vice president for such-and-such corporation. Then he asked what I did. Without giving it a second's thought, I answered:

"I am a lover."

Thinking he had trouble understanding me through my accent, he said, "You mean *a foreigner*?"

"No," I said, smiling. "A lover."

During the course of our conversation, I told him that I was traveling to meet with Muslim leaders in Pakistan, which startled him.

"Why?"

"Because of the Father's love for them."

Which startled him even more. And for the next eight hours that is all we talked about.

It is, in fact, all that I *want* to talk about. I am a lover, and I will forever stay a lover. It is not only my identity, it is my responsibility. When others want to talk about doctrine, I want to talk about the Father's love. When others want to talk about morality, I want to talk about the Father's love. When others want to talk about politics, I want to talk about the Father's love.

This will come as no surprise, but of all the disciples, John is my favorite. He is my favorite because he was the one closest to Jesus' heart, the one who loved Him the dearest, who followed Him the closest. Of the 12, he was the only one to be with Jesus at the Cross. It was there that John saw the clearest and most compelling definition of love. Like a barely-living butterfly impaled by a collector's straight pin, Jesus was impaled by a crucifier's nails, His life dissolving, His liquid draining out of Him to pool in the hearts of those who loved Him. It was a baptism of love for John, I think. A *bloody* baptism. If you read John's Gospel and his epistles, they are all about love. He is often referred to as "the apostle of love." Later in his life, he spoke on almost nothing else.

There is a story told about John being criticized by one of his own disciples, saying, "Why don't you talk about anything else?"

To which he replied: "Because there isn't anything else."[2]

Getting Personal

This Jesus, the very incarnation of love, saw people through Heaven's eyes. In doing so, some were ennobled; others were enraged. The sinners He dined with were honored. The scribes, who were taking note of the guest list, were horrified. Luke records one such dinner party:

Then all the tax collectors and the sinners drew near to Him to hear Him. And the Pharisees and scribes complained, saying, "This Man receives sinners and eats with them" (Luke 15:1-2).

The loveless one sees only the caterpillar, while the lover sees the butterfly.

Whose eyes do *you* want to have? The eyes of the critic...or the eyes of Christ?

If you answered as I think you did, be prepared to receive what Christ received—*criticism*. He was criticized for seeing others through Heaven's eyes. *I* am sometimes criticized for doing the same. And so will you be. Some people will love you for it; others will loathe you. And the loathing will likely come from the very religious.

Sue Monk Kidd talks about the different responses she experienced from people who had seen the transformation that had taken place in her. She talks about the critic and the effect the critic had on her.

Sometimes people are happy with our wings and support the unfurling. Sometimes, though, they're afraid of our wings and try to talk us back into the old larval life.

They can ignore our wings, tolerate them, attack them, applaud them, or bless them. They may even be changed by them. A transformation in one member of the family often creates transformation in others. Sometimes they go weave their own cocoons and join us. In *Hope for the Flowers,* the caterpillar Yellow was concerned about what would happen if she became a butterfly and her close friend Stripe remained a caterpillar. A gray-haired caterpillar told her, "If you change, you can fly and show him how beautiful butterflies are. Maybe he will want to become one too!"

I encountered all sorts of reactions to the changes in my life. When the reaction was negative, I sometimes went into a temporary tailspin, regressed, and questioned everything.

The best advice I received on this subject was from another older woman who'd been through many cocoons and many pairs of wings. I told her, "People won't let me change." (As if people could really do that.) What I was actually saying was, "I'm afraid of people's reaction to my changes." The woman touched my cheek with her hand and said, *"Love your wings."*[3]

When you finish this chapter, I want you to take some time and prayerfully reflect on your life and what God is doing in you. In preparation for that, I want to leave you with this thought:

You can listen to the criticism of caterpillars.

Or, you can love your wings.

You can crawl back into your cocoon.

Or, you can fly.

In flying, you can show the world how beautiful butterflies truly are. And maybe, just maybe, some of those caterpillars will want to become butterflies, too!

THE READER'S PRAYER

Dear Father,

How I long to see people the way You see them.

Give me eyes to see all the beauty that is emerging everywhere around me.

Help me to believe that there is a butterfly struggling to emerge from the gooey mess in all of our lives.

Help me to believe in that butterfly, hope in that butterfly, love that butterfly.

Thank You for the process of transformation, and for being with me in the pain of that process.

Don't stop with the process, Lord, until the beauty of who You created me to be emerges, fully formed and ready to fly.

Grant me the courage to rise above the earthbound criticism that comes from so many religious people and manages to worm its way into my life.

Help me to love my wings.

I pray about the present circumstances in my life, full of darkness and pain that seems not only confining but confusing.

Give me eyes to see what You are doing in me.

Help me to understand.

And where I can't understand, help me to trust.

CHAPTER 8

SEEING JESUS THROUGH HEAVEN'S EYES

*And suddenly a voice came from heaven, saying, "**This is My beloved Son, in whom I am well pleased**"* (Matthew 3:17).

*Yet I have set My King on My holy hill of Zion. I will declare the decree: The LORD has said to Me, "**You are My Son**, today I have begotten You. Ask of Me, and I will give You the nations for Your inheritance, and the ends of the earth for Your possession"* (Psalm 2:6-8).

*Behold! My Servant whom I uphold, My Elect One **in whom My soul delights!** I have put My Spirit upon Him; He will bring forth justice to the Gentiles* (Isaiah 42:1).

SEEING A KING IN SERVANT'S CLOTHING

The biblical revelation of the Messiah was like a slow-developing Polaroid®, except instead of taking minutes to develop, it took millennia. First it was just a little square of white nothingness, not even a hint of a picture—no lines, no color, no dimension. Then, as you squint at it, a few lines begin to form a shape—sketchy and shadowy, faceless and featureless—but a definite shape. You hold it in your hand, waiting. And as you wait, the random lines outline a figure. And the figure gets filled in with color. A face develops. The color spreads, deepening as it does. Soon the photo has dimension, and eventually, the picture is fully developed.

Try looking at the developing picture of the Messiah, not through the eyes of a modern-day believer but through eyes of an ancient-day believer. Imagine trying to figure out whose picture it was. Imagine trying to figure out where He was coming from, when He would get here, and what He would do when He did.

The picture of the Promised One developed slowly, simply, and sublimely.

Ever since Adam's and Eve's Fall from innocence, the world had been on its knees, folding its hands in a collective prayer, eagerly awaiting its Savior. Here and there hints of His coming could be sensed, like the fragrance of faraway flowers in the sigh of a late afternoon. Now and then rumors of *how* and *when* and *who* could be heard rustling through the pages of the Old Testament, like fallen leaves before a gust of autumn wind.

The Savior would come from the seed of the woman, we are told (see Gen. 3:15). Eve, mother of all the living, would start the promised line that would one day culminate in the hope of the world (see Luke 3:23-39). He would come through the unlikeliest of sources—an old man, past the age of fathering children, and a barren woman, without the fertility to conceive one (see Gen. 12:1-3). The birth of every baby boy kept the promise alive. Could it be *him*? Could *he* be the one? The *coming one*? The one who would bring the world back to Eden? The one who would restore all that had been lost?

Little by little these sketchy lines of revelation converged to form discernible features, and a portrait of the Promised One began to emerge. He would be born in Bethlehem (see Mic. 5:2-5) of a virgin (see Isa. 7:14) and ascend David's throne as king (see Isa. 9:7), whose reign was pictured as a return to Eden, where the wolf would dwell with the lamb…and the lion would eat straw like the ox…and a nursing child would play by a cobra's hole and not be hurt (see Isa. 11:1-9).

The picture is slow in developing, but it is clear in developing. When we get deeper into Isaiah, though, the picture gets blurred. In several passages Isaiah clearly pictures the promised Messiah as an exalted king. In other passages, though, he pictures him as a lowly servant, and a suffering servant at that—one that is despised, rejected, and executed (see Isa. 52:13–53:12).

This confused Jewish scholars. They knew something about the king and his lineage. They knew who the king's forefathers were, what land he would come from, what his kingdom would look like. But who was this unnamed servant of unknown origin?

Looking back, it is easy for us to see that the two pictures reveal the same person. The picture of the lowly servant reveals Jesus at His first coming, and the picture of the exalted king reveals Jesus at His second coming. Jewish scholars, however, knew nothing of two comings, and they couldn't fit the two pictures together. Consequently, they viewed the disparate portraits as referring to different people.

The Jewish nation had expected a king, a mighty king who would topple whatever kingdoms oppressed it, and, in doing so, usher in the Kingdom of God. What they got was indeed a king, but He was a king in servant's clothing, meek and lowly, who came not to be served but to serve. And *this* they were *not* prepared for—which is why Jesus became a stumbling block to so many of them.

In Matthew 3:17, the Father brings these two pictures together. He doesn't place them side by side though. Instead, He superimposes the one over the other. He takes the picture of the royal son of Psalm 2:7: *"The LORD has said to Me, 'You are My Son, today I have begotten You.'"* And on top of it He places the picture of the lowly servant of Isaiah 42:1: *"Behold! My Servant whom I uphold, My Elect One in whom My soul delights!"* In doing so, God is saying that the two pictures are not two people but rather one.

Here is the point. Only Kingdom eyes could see a king in servant's clothing. Only Kingdom eyes could see the heir to David's throne cradled in a feeding trough, surrounded by barn animals. Only Kingdom eyes could see the prince in the pauper. The shepherds had them. Luke says that after they left the stable where Jesus was born, the shepherds returned to their flocks, glorifying and praising God for all the things that they had heard and *seen* (see Luke 2:20). So did the Magi, who *saw* the Child with Mary His mother; and they fell down and worshipped Him (see Matt. 2:11). And so did Zacharias, who prophesied that this child was the promised deliverer (see Luke 1:67-79). And Simeon, when he took the baby Jesus in his arms and proclaimed that ***"my eyes have seen** Your salvation"* (Luke 2:30).

Only Kingdom eyes could see Him then.

Only Kingdom eyes can see Him now.

And why is that important? Because the King who came to so many people *then* is the same King who comes to so many of us *now*. He comes in ways that will surprise us, even shock us, if we're not used to seeing God cooing in a manger or crying out from a Cross. He comes to us in ways that will seem scandalous if we're not used to seeing royalty hobnob with riff-raff. He comes to us in ways that will seem sacrilegious if we're not used to seeing law trumped by grace and judgment by mercy.

The King comes to us in ways that take Kingdom eyes in order to see. Otherwise we would look for Him in the palaces of the mighty and overlook Him in the barns of the lowly. We would look for Him among the pious in the synagogues, not among the prostitutes on the streets. He comes with His identity cloaked. He comes to us in the ragged lives of the poor, for instance, among the threadbare and the footsore, shuffling toward us with outstretched hands. He comes to us in the one who is hungry for some crust of human kindness, in the one who is thirsty for some cool cup of companionship.

He comes to us in the wounded Jew and in the war-weary Muslim. He comes to us asking for the Father's love, although He will likely not say it in those words.

Will we give it, you and I?

Will we be bread to the hungry Christ, water to the thirsty Christ?

Will we be clothes to the naked Christ, friend to the lonely Christ?

Likely not…unless we can see past the clothes that conceal a King.

SEEING WITH KINGDOM EYES

Unless we are accustomed to seeing royalty in rags, we will likely not see our King in the plainly clothed moments of our everyday lives.

In John 3:3, Jesus tells Nicodemus that he can't even *see* the Kingdom unless he is born again. With our new birth we are given new eyes. And as we go from experiencing a birth conceived in love to a baptism drenched in love, our eyes develop even greater perspective—a Kingdom perspective. Eyes that see people on earth as they are in Heaven. Eyes that focus on their destiny rather than their history.

So exactly what *are* Kingdom eyes?

They are the eyes of a child. When the blind and lame were being healed by Jesus at the Temple, children in the Temple area were shouting, "Hosanna to the Son of David," but the chief priests and teachers of the law were indignant, saying, *"Do you hear what these children are saying?"* To which Jesus replied, quoting Psalm 8, *"Yes…have you never read, 'From the lips of children and infants You have ordained praise'?"* (Matt. 21:16 NIV).

How is it that children were the ones who recognized Jesus as the promised King when the chief priests and teachers of the law completely missed Him? Because children can see when an emperor has no clothes. They can also see when an emperor is concealed by his clothes. They can see, for example, that when Jesus entered Jerusalem riding bareback on a baby donkey, it was a regal scene, not a ridiculous one, the way some adults likely saw it.

Children were always dear to the Savior's heart, and on occasion He used them to illustrate spiritual truths. In settling a dispute with His disciples about who was the greatest in God's Kingdom, for example, Jesus called a little child and had him stand among them.

> *And He said, "I tell you the truth, unless you change and become like little children, you will never enter the kingdom of heaven. Therefore, whoever humbles himself like this child is the greatest in the kingdom of heaven"* (Matthew 18:3-4 NIV).

One important lesson I learned from my spiritual father, Jack Taylor, is that the Kingdom of God is not about achieving but receiving. Adults are great at achieving but poor at receiving. Children, on the other hand, are poor at achieving but great at receiving.

E. Stanley Jones has this to say about receiving as it relates to the Kingdom:

> Be poor enough to receive and everything is open to you, above all the very Kingdom of Heaven belongs to you. Not that you belong to the Kingdom of Heaven—you do—but more astonishing still, the Kingdom of Heaven belongs to you—all its resources, all its forgiveness, all its power, all its everything belongs to you if only you are poor enough to receive it.[1]

There is nothing poorer than a child, nothing dearer than a child, and, according to Jesus, nothing greater in the Kingdom of Heaven.

Frederick Buechner (pronounced "beekner"), in his book, *The Magnificent Defeat,* explains why children were so dear to Jesus and why they were so clearly an illustration of Kingdom qualities:

> A child has not made up his mind yet about what is and what is not possible. He has no fixed preconceptions about what reality is; and if someone tells him that the mossy place under the lilac bush is a magic place, he may wait until he thinks that no one is watching him, but then he will very probably crawl in under the lilac bush to see for himself. A child also knows how to accept a gift. He does not worry about losing his dignity or becoming indebted if he accepts it. His conscience does not bother him because the gift is free and he has not earned it and therefore really has no right to it. He just takes it, with joy. In fact, if it is something that he wants very much he may even ask for it. And lastly, a child knows how to trust. It is late at night and very dark and there is the sound of sirens as his father wakes him. He does not explain anything but just takes him by the hand and gets him up, and the child is scared out of his wits and he has no idea what is going on, but he takes his father's hand anyway and lets his father lead him wherever he chooses in the darkness.[2]

These are the qualities that make children the greatest in the Kingdom of Heaven. And all the wealth and resources, all the power and authority of that Kingdom are ours—if only we stretch out our weak, little hands to receive them.

Now back to the theme of humility that Jesus uses when He places the boy in front of the crowd. Read these words by Colin Urquhart, who expresses it beautifully:

> To understand he is a child of the Kingdom with all the resources of heaven available to him, places within man's reach such infinite power and riches that can only be entrusted to

those who are prepared to submit their lives to the King. Such resources could not be made available to those who would abuse such gifts.[3]

The gifts are so great that only the backs of the weak are able to bear them (see 2 Cor. 12:9). And there is no weaker back than that of a child.

SEEING THE KINGDOM OF HEAVEN

From the time of His baptism to the time of His ascension, Jesus spoke of one thing—the good news of the Kingdom (see Matt. 4:23). *That*, He tells us, is what He was sent to do (see Luke 4:43). And He sent out His disciples to do the same (see Luke 9:1-2). The phrase "Kingdom of God" or its equivalent is used 101 times in the New Testament. The prayer that Jesus taught His disciples to pray begins and ends with it (compare Matt. 6:10 with 6:13). The Beatitudes begin and end with it (compare Matt. 5:3 with 5:10). The ministry of Jesus itself begins and ends with the Kingdom of God (compare Matt. 4:17 with Acts 1:3).

Jesus was obsessed with the Kingdom. And rightly so. He had just come from Heaven where the Kingdom stood in all its splendor, everything radiant in its beauty, everything in harmony with the love of God, everything at peace, everything bursting with life, brimming with joy. For Him, *that* was the *real* world. Earth, even at its best, was merely a dim and distorted reflection of all that existed in Heaven.

How does Jesus explain that Kingdom in ways we can understand? To borrow from C.S. Lewis, it is like trying to explain to a child what a holiday at the sea would be like when the child has never even heard of the ocean, let alone seen it—never splashed in its surf, never built sandcastles on its shore, never gone beachcombing for sea shells. At times, Jesus almost seemed at a loss for literal words to describe the Kingdom, and He resorted to images that were more familiar to His audience.

The kingdom of heaven is like a mustard seed, which a man took and sowed in his field, which indeed is the least of all the seeds; but when it is grown it is greater than the herbs and becomes a tree, so that the birds of the air come and nest in its branches (Matthew 13:31-32).

The kingdom of heaven is like treasure hidden in a field, which a man found and hid; and for joy over it he goes and sells all that he has and buys that field (Matthew 13:44).

The kingdom of heaven is like a merchant seeking beautiful pearls, who, when he had found one pearl of great price, went and sold all that he had and bought it (Matthew 13:45-46).

The story of the Bible is the story of God establishing His rule on earth as it is in Heaven. His first co-rulers were Adam and Eve, who were put here to govern, exercising dominion and spreading His Kingdom by multiplying His image throughout the earth. When they failed a test of their loyalty, war broke out on earth. And the world has been at war ever since. The rest of biblical history is a record of patriarchs, priests, prophets, and kings whom God raised up to re-establish His rule. In the Book of Revelation, we see the climactic battle played out, Paradise regained, and the Kingdom of God finally and gloriously established on earth.

E. Stanley Jones in his excellent book on the Kingdom, titled, *The Unshakable Kingdom and the Unchanging Person,* explains why Jesus used illustrations instead of definitions.

Jesus didn't define the Kingdom in precise terms, perhaps because He was the definition. We may define the Kingdom since He has shown us what it is—shown us in His own person, as: *The Kingdom of God is God's total order, expressed as realm and reign, in the individual and in society....*[4]

Jones also writes:

In the physical universe the same laws are seen in the cell and in the farthest star, the universe has marks of one creative God upon it—it is a universe and not a multiverse. Then the plan for the universe must be one plan—valid and vital for all men everywhere.[5]

If that is true, the Kingdom of God is comprehensive. It governs our thoughts and our actions. It governs how we work and how we play. It governs what we say and how we say it. It governs our marriage and our family. It governs our friendships and our finances. It governs how we forgive and how often, which is freely and always. The Kingdom of God is comprehensive health care for the soul—and not only for the soul, but for society. Nothing lies outside its jurisdiction. It covers all; it governs all.

One plan. One person. One priority.

The plan? The Kingdom of God. The person? Its King. The priority? Seeking first the Kingdom of God and its righteousness.

With that plan we are promised comprehensive care. Seek first the Kingdom of God and its righteousness, which is enfleshed in its King, and that will be the best social security you could ever want. Conversely, if that is not our priority, all bets are off, as William Law, English cleric and author wrote: "If you have not chosen the Kingdom of God first, it will in the end make no difference what you have chosen instead."[6]

When Jesus said that the Kingdom of God is *"within you"* (Luke 17:21), He was saying that it is embedded in our soul as deeply as our DNA is embedded in our body. We were made for it, and it, for us. It is in our blood, so to speak. When we live in harmony with its principles, wonderful things happen. Heaven comes down. Edens spring up, and everywhere wildernesses are transformed into oases, especially the wilderness of the human heart.

In his book, *The Clown in the Belfry,* Frederick Buechner writes:

We cannot make the Kingdom of God happen, but we can put out leaves as it draws near. We can be kind to each other. We can be kind to ourselves. We can drive back the darkness a little. We can make green places within ourselves and among ourselves where God can make His Kingdom happen.[7]

SEEING THE KINGDOM IN CHRIST

Have you ever seen the photographic technique known as *photo-mosaics?* It was developed by a photographer named Robert Silvers. I'm sure you've seen some of his work in bookstores. He takes a number of smaller photographs, copies them into a computer, and a software program arranges them into a mosaic that reveals a larger picture. He might have a larger picture of the Mona Lisa, for example, and if you look through a magnifying glass at the smaller pictures that make up the Mona Lisa, you'll find they are mostly photos of Leonardo da Vinci's sketches and artwork.

E. Stanley Jones wrote that "the character of that kingdom is seen in the character of Jesus—the Kingdom is Christlikeness universalized."[8] To illustrate what Jones meant, imagine the Kingdom of God as a photo-mosaic. As you step back from it, you see an expansive panorama of that Kingdom, shimmering in its glory. But when you step closer, and you put a magnifying glass to the smaller photos, you see that each one is a different picture of Christ. One, perhaps, when He is riding on a donkey into Jerusalem. Another when He is healing a blind man, and so forth.

What we have in the Beatitudes is a photomosaic of the Kingdom, composed of smaller photos of the character of Christ.

And seeing the multitudes, He went up on a mountain, and when He was seated His disciples came to Him. Then He opened His mouth and taught them, saying: "Blessed are the poor in spirit, for theirs is the kingdom of heaven. Blessed are those who mourn, for they shall be comforted. Blessed are the meek, for they shall inherit the earth. Blessed are those who hunger and thirst for righteousness, for they shall be filled. Blessed are the merciful, for they shall obtain mercy. Blessed are the pure in heart, for they shall see God. Blessed are the peacemakers, for they shall be called sons of God. Blessed are those who are persecuted for righteousness' sake, for theirs is the kingdom of heaven. Blessed are you when they revile and persecute you, and say all kinds of evil against you falsely for My sake. Rejoice and be exceedingly glad, for great is your reward in heaven, for so they persecuted the prophets who were before you" (Matthew 5:1-12).

Look closer and see if you don't see Jesus in those smaller pictures.

He was poor in spirit. Though Jesus was rich, the Scriptures tell us, yet for our sakes he became poor (see 2 Cor. 8:9). Though He existed in the form of God, He did not regard equality with God a thing to be grasped, but emptied Himself, taking on the form of a bondservant (see Phil. 2:3-8). He impoverished Himself—from His birth, where He clothed Himself in our flesh; to His baptism, where He identified Himself with our sin; to His crucifixion, where He died for our sin.

He mourned. Jesus was a man of sorrows acquainted with grief (see Isa. 53:3), weeping over the physical death of a friend He loved (see John 11:35), and later, over the spiritual death of a city He loved (see Luke 13:34).

He was meek. "*Take My yoke upon you and learn from Me,*" Jesus said to His followers, "*for I am gentle and humble in heart*" (Matt. 11:29 NIV). Paul uses the meekness of Christ as the basis for his appeal to the church at Corinth. "*Now I, Paul, myself urge you by the meekness and gentleness of Christ*" (2 Cor. 10:1 NASB). And when Jesus went to the Cross, He didn't go kicking and screaming but rather meekly and silently, "*like a lamb that is led to slaughter*" (Isa. 53:7 NASB).

He hungered and thirsted for righteousness. Jesus sought the Kingdom of God and its righteousness like a sun-struck man in the desert, His lips parched, His stomach gnawing with hunger. Doing His Father's will was His daily bread (see John 4:34). It was also His drink (see Luke 22:42). So strict was He about His diet that He refused the bread offered Him by satan when He was in the wilderness (see Matt. 4:3-4) and the wine offered Him by a soldier when He was on the Cross (see Matt. 27:33-34).

He was merciful. Other people's pain always touched His heart. Whether the solitary figure of the widow of Nain, who lost her only son (see Luke 7:11-15), or the downcast multitudes, who were like sheep without a shepherd (see Matt. 9:36), Jesus felt compassion for them all, and He showed mercy to them all.

He was pure in heart. Jesus was the Lamb of God (see John 1:29), without spot or blemish (see Heb. 9:14), holy, innocent, and undefiled (see Heb. 7:26).

He was a peacemaker. Paul tells us that God was in Christ reconciling the world (see 2 Cor. 5:19) and that it was the Father's good pleasure to reconcile all things to Himself, *"having made peace through the blood of His cross"* (Col. 1:20 NASB).

The composite of Jesus we see in the Beatitudes forms a picture of the Kingdom of God. For the Kingdom is merely the character of Christ as it is lived out in the everyday moments of His life. Take all the qualities of His life—His love, His joy, His peace, His justice, His mercy, His kindness, His righteousness, His wisdom—and fill every individual with them, as well as every institution, and you have God's will being done on earth as it is in Heaven.

And everywhere we go, when we take Jesus with us, His Kingdom comes along, with all its power. In his book, *The Clown in the Belfry*, Frederick Buechner comments on the nature of this power:

> The power which is in Jesus, and before which all other powers on earth and in Heaven give way, the power that holds all things in existence from the sparrow's eye to the farthest star, is above all else a loving power. That means we are loved

even in our lostness. That means we are precious, every one of us, even as we pass on the street without so much as noticing each other's faces. Every city is precious. The world is precious. Someday the precious time will be up for each of us. But the Kingdom of God is at hand. Nothing is different and everything is different. It reaches out to each of our precious hands while there's still time.

Repent and believe in the gospel, Jesus says. Turn around and believe that the good news that we are loved is gooder than we ever dared hope, and that to believe in that good news, is of all glad things in the world the gladdest thing of all.[9]

Amen, and come, Lord Jesus.

THE READER'S PRAYER

Our Father in heaven, hallowed be Your name. Your kingdom come. Your will be done on earth as it is in heaven. Give us this day our daily bread. And forgive us our debts, as we forgive our debtors. And do not lead us into temptation, but deliver us from the evil one. For Yours is the kingdom and the power and the glory forever. Amen (Matthew 6:9-13).

CHAPTER 9

SEEING YOUR ENEMIES
THROUGH HEAVEN'S EYES

When Jesus had said these things, He was troubled in spirit, and testified and said, "Most assuredly, I say to you, one of you will betray Me." Then the disciples looked at one another, perplexed about whom He spoke. Now there was leaning on Jesus' bosom one of His disciples, whom Jesus loved. Simon Peter therefore motioned to him to ask who it was of whom He spoke. Then, leaning back on Jesus' breast, he said to Him, "Lord, who is it?" Jesus answered, "It is he to whom I shall give a piece of bread when I have dipped it." And having dipped the bread, He gave it to Judas Iscariot, the son of Simon. Now after the piece of bread, Satan entered him. Then Jesus said to him, "What you do, do quickly" (John 13:21-27).

"Simon, Simon, Satan has asked to sift all of you as wheat. But I have prayed for you, Simon, that your faith may not fail. And when you have turned back, strengthen your brothers." But he replied, "Lord, I am ready to go with You to prison and to death." Jesus answered, "I tell you, Peter, before the rooster crows today, you will deny three times that you know Me" (Luke 22:31-34 NIV).

When Jesus' followers saw what was going to happen, they said, "Lord, should we strike with our swords?" And one of them struck the servant of the high priest, cutting off his right ear. But Jesus answered, "No more of this!" And He touched the man's ear and healed him (Luke 22:49-51 NIV).

When they came to the place called the Skull, there they crucified Him, along with the criminals—one on His right, the other on His left. Jesus said, "Father, forgive them, for they do not know what they are doing." And they divided up His clothes by casting lots (Luke 23:33-34 NIV).

THE KING'S TEACHING

In the Sermon on the Mount, Jesus gave His first recorded teaching on the Kingdom of God. When He finished, Matthew says the crowd that heard it was amazed. G.K. Chesterton, the British essayist who was a contemporary of C.S. Lewis, described the sermon like this:

> On the first reading of the Sermon on the Mount you feel it turns everything upside down, but the second time you read it, you discover that it turns everything right side up. The first time you read it you feel that it is impossible, but the second time, you feel that nothing else is possible.[1]

Chesterton's words are particularly applicable to the upside-down way that Jesus tells us to treat our enemies. Let's look at a few of those "impossible" ideals.

The first passage is in Luke 6:27-31:

But I say to you who hear: Love your enemies, do good to those who hate you, bless those who curse you, and pray for those who spitefully use you. To him who strikes you on the one cheek, offer the other also. And from him who takes away your cloak, do not withhold your tunic either. Give to everyone who asks of you. And from him who takes away your goods do not ask them back. And just as you want men to do to you, you also do to them likewise.

In his book, *The Unshakable Kingdom and the Unchanging Person*, E. Stanley Jones takes a first look at Jesus' advice, does a double-take, then looks at it again, this time through Kingdom eyes:

> Love your enemies, turn the other cheek, and go the second mile when compelled to go one. Impossible idealism—you would be everybody's doormat, everyone would walk on you. Would they? The aim of a quarrel is to get rid of your enemy. Suppose you strike back and give blow for blow. Do you get rid of your enemy? You fix the enmity by every blow you give. By turning the other cheek you disarm your enemy. He hits you on the cheek and you, by your moral audacity, hit him on the heart by turning the other cheek. His enmity is dissolved. Your enemy is gone. You get rid of your enemy by getting rid of your enmity.[2]

The second passage I want you look at is in Matthew's version of the sermon in chapter 5, verses 21-24:

> *You have heard that it was said to those of old, "You shall not murder, and whoever murders will be in danger of the judgment." But I say to you that whoever is angry with his brother without a cause shall be in danger of the judgment. And whoever says to his brother, "Raca!" shall be in danger of the council. But whoever says, "You fool!" shall be in danger of hell fire. Therefore if you bring your gift to the altar, and there remember that your brother has something against you, leave your gift there before the altar, and go your way. First be reconciled to your brother, and then come and offer your gift.*

Dietrich Bonhoeffer, in his book, *The Cost of Discipleship*, offers some sobering reflections on those words:

The angry word is a blow struck at our brother, a stab at his heart: it seeks to hit, to hurt and to destroy. A deliberate insult is even worse, for we are then openly disgracing our brother in the eyes of the world, and causing others to despise him. With our hearts burning with hatred, we seek to annihilate his moral and material existence. We are passing judgment on him, and that is murder. And the murderer will himself be judged.[3]

The final passage I want you to consider is Matthew 5:43-45:

You have heard that it was said, "You shall love your neighbor and hate your enemy." But I say to you, love your enemies, bless those who curse you, do good to those who hate you, and pray for those who spitefully use you and persecute you, that you may be sons of your Father in heaven; for He makes His sun rise on the evil and on the good, and sends rain on the just and on the unjust.

In his book, *Strength to Love,* Martin Luther King Jr. gives a globally relevant admonition based on Jesus' words:

Returning hate for hate multiplies hate, adding deeper darkness to a night already devoid of stars. Darkness cannot drive out darkness; only light can do that. Hate cannot drive out hate; only love can do that. Hate multiplies hate, violence multiplies violence, and toughness multiplies toughness in a descending spiral of destruction. So when Jesus says "Love your enemies," he is setting forth a profound and ultimately inescapable admonition. Have we not come to such an impasse in the modern world that we must love our enemies—or else? The chain reaction of evil—hate begetting hate, wars producing more wars—must be broken, or we shall be plunged into the dark abyss of annihilation.[4]

This book is about the Father's love, about how He brought the world into existence as a stage upon which that love could be seen, heard, and felt by all. No one was excluded. For God so loved *the world* that He gave His only Son that *whosoever* should believe in Him would not perish but have everlasting life.

God so loved—not Americans, not Jews, not Christians, not Republicans—the *world*. He doesn't want anyone to perish but wants everyone to come to repentance (see 2 Pet. 3:9). *Everyone.* The Father's heart is for the Jew *and* the Gentile, for the slave *as well as* the free, for the woman *along with* the man. And that includes Muslims, whom many believe are our enemies. Muslims are not a problem but a promise. Although a covenant was made with Isaac, a promise was made to Ishmael. God did not look out for Sarah and look away from Hagar. When Sarah kicked Hagar out of their camp, Hagar was forced to fend for herself in the wilderness. With her son on the brink of death, she cried out to God, sat down in a heap, and wept. God heard her cries, saw her tears, and sent assurance through an angel that the boy would not die but multiply and father a great nation (see Gen. 21:8-21).

The God of the Bible is a searching God, seeking to find us, regardless of how alone we feel or how afflicted we are. It doesn't seem to matter where we have ended up or how we have gotten there. It doesn't matter into what physical wilderness we have wandered or into what spiritual wilderness we have sought refuge. All that matters is that we are found and that we are brought home. The parables of the lost sheep, the lost coin, and the lost son all tell the same story—the story of how greatly we are loved, how greatly we are missed, and how happy Heaven is when we are found and brought home (see Luke 15).

That includes our enemies.

Take Saul of Tarsus, for example—a terrorist in the eyes of the early church, a jihadist against this emerging threat to his Jewish faith. He was a murderer, and he took pride in the fact that he did his murderous duty with such religious zeal (see Acts 9:1-2). From the perspective of the early church, Saul was seen as an enemy. But that is not the way Heaven saw him. Heaven saw him as a friend in the making.

There are a lot of ways an enemy can be dealt with. He can be threatened into silence. He can be tortured into compliance. He can be imprisoned or exiled, even murdered. Jesus does none of those things. Instead, Jesus seeks him out—not to censure him, not to intimidate him, not to harm him, but to love him. And in loving him, Jesus turned this most feared of enemies into the most faithful of friends. Look in Acts 9. Put yourself into the scene, looking with Kingdom eyes and hearing with Kingdom ears. What do you see? What do you hear?

> *As he journeyed he came near Damascus, and suddenly a light shone around him from heaven. Then he fell to the ground, and heard a voice saying to him, "Saul, Saul, why are you persecuting Me?" And he said, "Who are You, Lord?" Then the Lord said, "I am Jesus, whom you are persecuting"* (Acts 9:3-5).

What do you see? You see a light—not fire, not brimstone—but a heavenly light, dispelling the hellish darkness that had blackened Saul's heart. And what do you hear? You hear a voice. There is no anger in it, no animosity, no antagonism. But there is tenderness in it, tenderness tinged with sadness. "Saul, Saul...." The repetition of the name is reminiscent of His words to Martha when she came out of the kitchen, angry at her sister and at Jesus, accusing Him of not caring that she had left her to do the serving alone. "Martha, Martha," He begins. And you can hear the tenderness in His voice, mingled with sadness. He doesn't return her anger with anger. He corrects her, but in the gentlest of ways, without a critical spirit or a condescending tone (see Luke 10:38-42). Then there is His final entry into Jerusalem the week before He is to be crucified. He weeps as the holy city comes into view. He weeps not for His destruction but for hers. And the words He speaks have that same tender but grieving tone. "Jerusalem, Jerusalem..." (see Matt. 23:37).

After Jesus calls Saul by name, He doesn't threaten him, doesn't rebuke him, doesn't lecture him. There is no ridicule, no payback, no evening of the score. Just a tender, sorrowful question. "Why?" And it sounds as if Jesus is confused, at a loss to understand all the animosity that Saul has had for Him. *"Why are you persecuting Me?"*

That was the beginning of their friendship—Jesus seeking out an enemy, and loving him instead of hating him, forgiving him instead of punishing him, blessing him instead of cursing him.

Before then, Saul was filled with hate for Jesus and for anyone who followed Him. His hate was an obsession. Blaise Pascal once said that "men never commit evil so fully and so joyfully as when they do it for religious convictions." The bloody history of the world's religions backs up Pascal's claim. The three great Abrahamic religions—Judaism, Christianity, and Islam—are stained with the blood of their enemies. Jews killing Christians. Christians killing Jews. Christians killing Muslims. Muslims killing Jews and Christians. Even within Christianity, there are times when Catholics killed Protestants and Protestants killed Catholics. And within Islam, times when Shiites kill Sunnis and Sunnis kill Shiites.

When will it all ever end? And if it doesn't end, where will it all lead?

Martin Luther King Jr. was right: "The chain reaction of evil—hate begetting hate, wars producing more wars—must be broken, or we shall be plunged into the dark abyss of annihilation."[5]

How can that chain reaction be broken?

By the radical principles that Jesus taught in the Sermon on the Mount—loving our enemy, forgiving our enemy, blessing our enemy.

However difficult it was to treat His enemies like that, Jesus practiced what He preached. He lived by those principles; He died by those principles. And in doing so, He showed the world how to step back from the abyss.

THE KING'S EXAMPLE

The idea of loving our enemies is hard for a lot of people to swallow. But even those who are the most skeptical of Jesus' claims and the most critical of Jesus' teaching have to admit—He took His own medicine. He took it without resisting the spoon, without complaining about the taste, and without adding the slightest bit of sugary sentimentality to help the medicine go down.

Follow the narrative of Jesus' last 24 hours, and see how He took it. What you see and hear is the best visual aid to the Sermon on the Mount you could ever find. Look and listen…and you will fall even more in love with Him than you are now.

Judas. Jesus chose him as one of the 12, all the while knowing that one day he would betray Him. For three and a half years, Jesus walked with him, talked with him, ate with him, ministered with him. He befriended one who would turn into an enemy when Jesus most needed a friend. That final night in the upper room, Jesus washed Judas' feet, just as He had done for the other disciples. He dined with the man who would soon turn the tables on Him. He spoke kindly to him, never once berating him for his betrayal. And He fed part of the Passover meal to him with His own hands, dismissing Judas in hushed tones so as not to publicly humiliate him in front of the other disciples (see John 13:21-30).

Peter. Jesus warned him ahead of time about his defection. To soften the blow, Jesus explained to Peter that it wasn't all his fault, that satan had a hand in it, too. For this man who would deny not only his friendship with Jesus but even his acquaintance with Him, Jesus prayed. He prayed, and He told Peter, essentially, not to let the failure destroy him, that He still loved him, still believed in him, still thought he was the right man for the job (see Luke 22:31-32). And after Jesus rose from the dead, He sought out Peter, especially Peter, because Peter especially needed to be found and brought home to the Savior's loving arms (see John 21:15-19).

Malchus. He was the high priest's servant who accompanied the soldiers when they arrested Jesus in the garden. In a rash move to defend Jesus, Peter drew his sword and cut off a portion of the servant's ear. Jesus' response?

Jesus said to him, "Put your sword in its place, for all who take the sword will perish by the sword. Or do you think that I cannot now pray to My Father, and He will provide Me with more than twelve legions of angels?" (Matthew 26:52-53)

What an incredible restraint of the angelic arsenal He had at His disposal! On His way to the Cross, Jesus wouldn't allow so much as a sword to be used in His defense. Nor would He let so much as an ear to be sacrificed on His behalf. Finally and beautifully, in His most miniscule but perhaps most regal of miracles, Jesus healed the ear of His enemy (see Luke 22:51).

The other disciples. Outmanned and out-armed, they deserted Jesus at His most desperate hour. His response? He didn't call them cowards; instead, He covered for them, explaining that their actions were simply a fulfillment of prophecy:

Then Jesus said to them, "All of you will be made to stumble because of Me this night, for it is written: 'I will strike the Shepherd, and the sheep of the flock will be scattered'" (Matthew 26:31).

The religious leaders who tried Him. They accused Jesus falsely and gathered witnesses to testify against Him, again falsely. They hit Him. His response? He didn't defend Himself, and He didn't denigrate *them*. Not returning insult for insult, or injury for injury, He took the fist, silently, bravely, and with a bold resignation that befits a king (see Mark 14:53-65).

The Roman soldiers. Brutal men, they mocked Jesus, draping His shoulders with a purple cape, thrusting a thorny crown into His scalp, and humiliating Him as they took turns beating Him. His response? Again, He took the blows, turned the other cheek, and did not resist the evil that propped Him up and pummeled Him (see Mark 15:16-20).

The crowd that surrounded Him at the Cross. They taunted Jesus, quoting Scriptures to Him, daring Him to prove Himself King, if indeed He *was* one. His response? He bore the daggers of ridicule, the spears of sarcasm. And He didn't throw them back. He took it all, and He took it with the nobility of a true king (see Mark 15:29-32).

The soldiers at the Cross. The ones who hammered the nails into His hands, His feet. The ones who raised the Cross into place. And the ones hunched over a pair of dice, gambling for His cloak. His response? Forgiveness. And not only that, listen to His plea bargain on their behalf: *"Then Jesus said, 'Father, forgive them, for they do not know what they do'"* (Luke 23:34). In other words, Jesus is telling the Father that if the soldiers could only see Him for who He really was, if they knew that He was indeed a king, indeed the Son of God, they would never have done this. Remarkable, when you think about it. Jesus not only forgives His enemies, He defends them.

The two thieves. When you compare the parallel accounts, you discover that both thieves cursed Jesus (see Mark 15:32; Luke 23:39-40). Never once did Jesus curse back. Instead, He gave a blessing to the one who asked to be remembered. The blessing? The man had just asked that Jesus remember Him when He got to His Kingdom. That's all. And Jesus gave him Paradise. *Paradise!* In a few hours of witnessing Jesus' response to His enemies, one of those enemies was transformed into a friend, and remained a friend forever (see Luke 23:42-43).

We are told that when Peter denied Jesus for the third time, a rooster crowed, reminding him of Jesus' words earlier that night. He turned and saw Jesus looking at him. What he saw were not the eyes of an enemy but the eyes of a friend. And when their eyes met, we are told that Peter went away, weeping bitterly (see Luke 22:60-62). The next day Peter likely approached the Cross, but from afar. He saw Jesus' enemies, teeth bared like a pack of wolves that had cornered its prey. He heard the insults, the taunts, the mocking, the cursing. And he saw Jesus' response to them, heard His words and the tone in which the words were spoken. Here is how the example of Jesus impacted him, inspiring his words to fellow believers who were undergoing persecution by *their* enemies:

For what credit is it if, when you are beaten for your faults, you take it patiently? But when you do good and suffer, if you take it patiently, this is commendable before God. For to this you were called, because Christ also suffered for us, leaving us an example, that you should follow His steps: "Who committed no sin, nor was deceit found in His mouth"; who, when He was reviled, did not revile in return; when He suffered, He did not threaten, but committed Himself to Him who judges righteously (1 Peter 2:20-23).

What Peter saw and heard that day, though it was from a distance as he stood on the periphery, cloaked in anonymity, changed him forever. How could it not? How could anyone not be changed if he or she only knew the story—the *whole* story—of just how much we are loved?

There is a beautiful story about a teenage girl who lived in the dark days of the Soviet empire, a regime that was an enemy of all that Jesus was and all that He taught. So great was the darkness that she had never been inside a church. She didn't know who Jesus was, hadn't even heard the name. Until one day a friend slipped her a contraband copy of the Gospel of Luke. Her response when finishing it?

"I fell in love with Him!"

When our enemies realize what a friend they have in Jesus, falling in love naturally follows. And when they fall in love with Jesus, they fall in love with everything He loves and every*one* He loves...which is a worldful.

THE KING'S HEART

On March 4, 1865, under heavy guard to protect him from his enemies, Abraham Lincoln walked onto the platform where he gave his Second Inaugural Address, barely a month before the Civil War ended. John Wilkes Booth, a struggling actor turned political activist, was in the audience that day, seething with anger. He hated Lincoln with a vengeance. That hatred led to a plot to assassinate the president, which he carried out on the evening of April 14, five days after the war's end.

Lincoln ended his speech with these words:

With malice toward none; with charity for all, with firmness in the right as God gives us to see the right, let us strive on to finish the work we are in, to bind up the nation's wounds, to care for him who shall have borne the battle, and for his widow, and his orphan, to do all which may achieve and cherish a just and lasting peace, among ourselves, and with all nations.[6]

His words are similar to the words Jesus used as He inaugurated His Kingdom in the Sermon on the Mount. Like Him, Lincoln was a peacemaker. Like many peacemakers—like Jesus—he was killed for it. I am also a peacemaker. I have received death threats from those who see me as an enemy. And I have received the criticism from those who see me as a friend to the enemy.

I first started seeing the Muslims through the Father's eyes when Randy Clark prophesied over me on June 6th of 1995, saying, "I don't know you but I can see over your life that you are like a bulldozer. God is calling you to prepare the way in unchartered territory. You are a forerunner and you are here to prepare the preparers for the coming of the Son of Man." He shared that I am an apostle with a calling to prepare nations who had never yet heard the Gospel of the Kingdom. Before that, I hadn't given much thought to Muslims, let alone much heart. They were for me an ideology to be feared, not individuals to be loved. Now I love them. I pray for them. I weep for them. I offer practical help to them. I visit them, staying in their homes, and they visit me, staying in mine. They let me into their homes and into their hearts. They welcome me into their mosques, not as a visiting tourist but as an honored guest.

Here are just two of the hundreds of encounters I have had with the Muslim world. One was at a restaurant in Pakistan with two young radicals. Both men dishonored me, saying ugly things about Jesus, about me, about my faith. Trying to understand their hatred, I asked a sincere question. "Why can a Christian become a Muslim, and we *don't* kill him, but if a Muslim becomes a Christian, you *do*?"

The question set them on edge. I could feel their anger, their hatred, and for a moment I thought they might slit my throat. The one man actually made a gesture of running his finger across his throat as if to say, "Look out. You may be next." The darkness in them proved stronger than the light that was in me. And I wilted. After an hour and a half, though, my love for them started to overcome their hate for me. And though I couldn't say they saw me as their best friend, I can say that they no longer saw me as their enemy.

Many times when I am in Arab nations, I am invited to meet with the country's top leaders. I recall one such meeting when I was sitting in an elaborate palace, conversing with three brilliant Muslims about Jesus. One of them had three doctorates and knew the Bible better than anyone in the room, including me.

He wanted to take us all on a journey to have an encounter with God. It was a little out of my comfort zone, but I wanted to honor him, so I agreed, following his instructions. After that, I spoke a little on the love of God, a concept that is foreign to them. Of the 99 attributes of Allah listed in the Koran, not one of them is love. They listened with the same respect that I gave them when I listened. In that environment of love and respect, the Holy Spirit spoke to me about someone in the room having severe pain in his leg. When I shared this, one of the men said it was him. I asked if I could pray for him. He agreed. I prayed, and the Holy Spirit healed him.

I try to create an environment of love, respect, and honor. When I do, wonderful things happen. The Holy Spirit seems to feel most welcome in that environment, most at home. And He *is* most at home in an atmosphere like that, because that is the atmosphere He is used to in Heaven.

I have gone to Pakistan and other Muslim countries numerous times. Each time I get more of the Father's heart for them. I go with no agenda. I don't try to convict them or convert them. That is Holy Spirit's responsibility, not mine. I go speaking the language of love—a language that doesn't need a translator, because it's a language the deaf can hear and the blind can see. I speak in a way that honors them and respects them, the same way that I would want them to speak to me. I listen with genuine interest, the same way I would want them to listen to me. It's really just a way of applying the Golden Rule, in which Jesus said, "Do unto others as you would have them do unto you" (see Matt. 7:12).

As I do unto them as I would have them do unto me, a remarkable thing happens. Those who once saw themselves as my enemy now see themselves as my friend.

WHY THERE ARE PLACES WHERE DARKNESS RULES THE DAY

I have two pictures that I look at constantly. One horrifies me; the other haunts me. I'll share the horrific one first; the haunting one I'll save until the end of the chapter. Sandwiched in between are two other pictures; one from a film, the other from a book. Both tragic. Both true.

The first picture is of a 13-year-old Christian girl on the cusp of puberty. She lived in Pakistan in a village near Cushawah. There she was raped by four Muslim men. I met her at the hospital where she was treated. She was covered with bruises and bloodied from the savage assault. My heart went out to her. Learning that she would get no help with the hospital bill, I paid it.

When she was released from the hospital, though, the oldest of her assailants, a prominent Muslim in the village, forced her to convert to Islam and marry him. In a tragically ironic twist to the story, because she was not a virgin at the time of her marriage, she was sentenced to death. Acid was poured down her throat and splashed onto her face, where it spilled over her body. The acid burned through the layers of her skin, and the flesh literally fell off in strips and sheets. She survived, but the scars left her looking like a ghoulish creature out of your worst nightmare.

Can you imagine having acid poured down your throat? The unbearable burning, eating away the tender tissue in your mouth, your esophagus, the lining of your stomach. There is nothing to put out the fire, nothing to stop the pain, the excruciating, unrelenting pain. And no sympathy from anyone—not from your family, not from your friends, not even from the hospital staff.

These are called "honor killings," as if to justify the barbarism. And they are a regular occurrence. If you visit a Middle Eastern country where the custom is practiced, you read about them in the daily newspaper, you hear about them in conversations with the locals, you see them on the nightly news.

If the concept is foreign to you, you can see an example of it in the film, *The Stoning of Soraya M.* It is based on a true story, written in 1990 by a French-Iranian journalist named Freidoune Sahebjam. The story of Soraya M. is about one of the victims of an "honor killing" in modern Iran. Her husband wants to find a way out of his marriage so he can marry a 14-year-old girl he is smitten with. But he can't afford to support two families or to return Soraya's dowry. When he learns that Soraya has been cooking meals for a recently widowed man, he finds justification for bringing her before the village authorities and falsely accuses her of adultery. Since women in their culture have few legal rights, can't stand up for themselves, and can't speak out against their husbands, she falls victim to an unappealable sentence of death by stoning.

On the day the sentence is to be carried out, she is buried up to her waist to prevent her from running away. The men of the village— including her husband and her two sons—execute the sentence. I would have thought they would use large stones, perhaps the size of grapefruits, that could knock someone out or put a mercifully quick end to their life.

But they used small stones, the size of a lime, even smaller. My guess is that smaller stones are used to prolong the torture.

It is a disturbing scene to watch, as one by one the stones hit her, graze her, cutting gashes on her face, her neck, her arms. The most difficult part is watching as her sons hesitate, then finally, though reluctantly, join in. The brutality seems to go on forever. Finally, she slumps to the ground in a lifeless heap.

The scene was not sensationalized; it was merely shown. This is how it is done—by men with small stones pelting the victim over and over until the sentence is carried out and honor is restored, with the husband free to marry to satisfy his lust of the month.

That is what it is like in many such villages. The man is king; his rule, absolute. He holds the power of life and death over every member of his family. But he holds it especially tightly and ruthlessly over the women in his family.

Then there is Souad's story. The title of her book is *Burned Alive: A Survivor of an "Honor Killing" Speaks Out*. She was raised an Arab woman in a tiny village on the West Bank. In telling her story, she tells the stories of other women. In this instance she talks about being beaten for falling asleep and letting the sheep wander home by themselves:

> I think we were beaten every day. A day without a beating was unusual.

> I think maybe it was this time that he [her father] tied me up, Kainat [her sister] and me, our hands behind our backs, our legs bound, and a scarf over our mouths to keep us from screaming. We stayed like that all night, tied to a gate in a big stable. We were with the animals, but we were worse off than they were.

> That is what it was like in our village. It was the law of men. The girls and the women were certainly beaten every day in

the other houses, too. You could hear the crying. It was not unusual to be beaten, to have your hair shaved off and be tied to a stable gate. There was no other way of living….[7]

The only hope for a woman was marriage. Even then it was a slender hope. Souad's mother married when she was 14, and had a child a year for the next 14 years. Only five are still living. One of them, a son, was treated, as all sons were, like royalty. Souad and her three sisters were allowed to live. The other girls were smothered immediately after they were born.

One of Souad's surviving sisters was later killed by her brother, Assad, who was upset with her and strangled her with a telephone cord. There was no sentence. No trial. No arrest. After all, he was a man. Police didn't investigate it. Friends didn't question it. Villagers didn't speak of it. After all, she was a woman. But Souad spoke of it, wrote of it, protested it. The woman was her sister. When she writes, she speaks of the violence as if it were a trade that fathers pass on to their sons, the younger generation serving as apprentices to the older.

As I said, Assad was violent like my father. He was a murderer, but that word doesn't have any meaning in my village when it comes to having a woman killed. It is the duty of the brother, the brother-in-law, or the uncle to preserve the family's honor. They have the right of life and death over their women. If the father or mother says to the son: "Your sister has sinned, you must kill her," he does it for the sake of honor and because it is the law….[8]

If you don't kill a girl who has dishonored the family, the people in the village will reject the family, and nobody will speak to the family or do business with them and the family will have to leave![9]

An important piece of the cultural puzzle, I thought as I read her words. There were reasons beyond honor—social and economic reasons.

Even so, it is hard to believe the level of barbarism such as the one in the following story.

> Being married was the most I could hope for in terms of free-
> dom. But even married, a woman risked her life at the least
> lapse in her conduct. I remember a woman who had four chil-
> dren. Her husband must have worked in the city, because he
> always had on a jacket. When I would see him in the distance
> he was always walking very fast, his shoes kicking up a storm
> of dust behind him. His wife's name was Souheila, and one
> day I heard my mother say that the village was telling stories
> about her. People thought she was involved with the owner
> of the store because she went there frequently to buy bread,
> vegetables, and fruit. Maybe she didn't have a big garden like
> ours or maybe she was seeing this man secretly, as my mother
> had done with Fadel. One day my mother said that her broth-
> ers had gone into her house and cut off her head. And that
> they had left the body on the ground and had walked around
> the village with her head. She also said that when her husband
> returned from his job he was happy to learn that his wife was
> dead since she'd been suspected of something with the store
> owner.[10]

Then it was her turn. Souad, hoping to marry her way out of a family that was no friend to women, especially single women, had her eye on
an eligible man in the village. They exchanged furtive glances, engaged
in surreptitious conversations, met in a sheltering wheat field, and it
was there that she became pregnant. The man was neither shamed, nor
shunned, nor sentenced. She, on the other hand, was.

After a family meeting, which she overheard, her brother-in-law vol-
unteered to be the one to restore the family's honor. The day the sentence
was to be carried out, her father and mother, brother and sisters, left her
alone in the house. That is when her brother-in-law entered the house
and doused her with gasoline. He lit a match, and she was immediately

engulfed in flames. Burned beyond recognition, she ran out of the house, flames trailing behind her. Somehow she survived. But another attempt on her life was made at the hospital. This time it was her mother bringing poison for her to drink. She was treated at the hospital, but treated minimally and resentfully. With help, she fled the country, never to see her family, her village, or the man she thought she loved again.

In another story she tells, this one about the murder of her sister-in-law, she reveals what I believe is the deep and tenacious root of this cultural problem.

> I saw Fatma [her sister-in-law] lying on the ground and my brother kicking her in the back. One day her eye was red and her face all blue. But you couldn't say or do anything. Between the father's violence and the son's, there was nothing for the rest of us to do but hide to avoid being beaten ourselves. Did my brother love his wife? For me love was a mystery. In our culture, you talk of marriage, not of love. Of obedience and total submission, not of a loving relationship between a man and a woman. Only the obligatory sexual relations with a virgin girl who had been bought for her husband. Where is love?[11]

Indeed. Where *is* it?

That is the nagging question I have asked myself every time I hear of an honor killing, a suicide bombing, a beheading, or other acts of barbarism.

In Donald Miller's book, *A Million Miles in a Thousand Years,* the author tells a story about a friend of his who had wrestled angrily with God about the genocide in Rwanda. Her name is Kathy, and the answer she received is a central piece of this cultural puzzle.

> Kathy took the tour bus to Ntarama. She walked into the church and looked at the bones lying cold on the iron rails. She looked at the ragged and bloody clothes hanging from the

walls. She was ready to feel the same old anger at God, only a thousandfold more. She was ready to pray her last prayer, announcing that she could no longer believe in God in a world with such pain, with so much devastation.

But Kathy told me it was then and there, in that church, that she heard from God. Instead of the old anger, she felt overwhelming tenderness and sorrow.

This is what happens when people walk away from Me, Kathy. I have brought you to this place to show you something important. This is what happens when My compassion and love leave a place. It is when people do not allow God to show up through them, she realized, that the world collapses in on itself.[12]

Jesus told His disciples to go to the far reaches of the world, sharing the love of God with everyone. It didn't matter whether they were Muslim or Jew, man or woman, slave or free. When we don't show up and let the light of God shine through us, *darkness rules.* When we don't show up and let the love of God show through us, *hatred rules.* When we don't show up and let the goodness of God spill from us, *evil rules.*

It's not that complicated.

Go, as Jesus commanded. And wherever you go—whether it is Pakistan or Pittsburgh—allow God to show up through you. When you and I don't, the world collapses in on itself.

It's that simple.

And that certain.

The final picture is of a Pakistani woman who was healed at one of my meetings where for the first time she experienced the love of God, the light of God, and the goodness of God. Her husband, who had died a year earlier, had experienced none of those things. He died in the darkness of his hatred, an enemy of so many and for so long. As the joy of her new life subsided, a seriousness came over her.

"How long have you known about this Jesus?" she asked.

I hesitated a second, then said, "Well, I'm from Norway, and we've known about Him there for some 1,000 years."

"And you?"

"Me, I've known Him most of my life, since I was eight."

She paused, collecting herself, then asked a question I'll never forget. "Why didn't you come sooner? If you had just come a year sooner, my husband might have come to know this Jesus, might have been healed by Him, and I would not be a widow."

As she spoke, I realized that what she said could be the epitaph on the tombstones of millions of Muslims, maybe tens of millions, hundreds of millions.

"Why didn't you come sooner?" The question chiseled itself into my memory. I'll never forget it, never forget *her*.

This woman, whom many would see as an enemy, became my friend through the mutual Friend we had in Jesus. *If I had loved Him more,* I thought, *I* **would** *have come sooner. If I had loved* **her** *more, her whom I once had thought of as an enemy, I would have come sooner.*

She is the reason I go back.

She is *always* the reason I go back.

The Reader's Prayer

(The Prayer of Saint Francis of Assisi)

Lord, make me an instrument of Your peace.

Where there is hatred, let me sow love; where there is injury, pardon; where there is doubt, faith; where there is despair, hope; where there is darkness, light; and where there is sadness, joy.

O Divine Master, grant that I may not so much seek to be consoled as to console; to be understood as to understand; to be loved as to love.

For it is in giving that we receive; it is in pardoning that we are pardoned; and it is in dying that we are born to eternal life.

Amen.

PART 4

SEEING THE FUTURE THE WAY THE FATHER SEES IT

The bridegroom in Solomon's Song of Songs is traditionally interpreted as God the lover of our souls. We are His bride. But His divine bridegroom says to the bride: "You are all fair, my love" (4:7). God says this to us! But how can it be true that we are "all fair" when we still struggle with sin? Is God blind? If not, then what He says is true. It is true as prophecy, a prophecy of our eternal identity and destiny. Christ refers to this when He says, "You, therefore, must be perfect, as your heavenly Father is perfect" (Matt. 5:48). God speaks from eternity and sees us as we are eternally before Him. To us this "all fair" perfection is only in the future. But to God everything is present. For that is what eternity is: not endless futures, but at all times actually present with no dead past or unborn future.... —Peter Kreeft[1]

CHAPTER 10

SEEING THE MINISTRY OF THE SPIRIT AND THE MYSTERY OF THE CHURCH

When the Day of Pentecost had fully come, they were all with one accord in one place. And suddenly there came a sound from heaven, as of a rushing mighty wind, and it filled the whole house where they were sitting. Then there appeared to them divided tongues, as of fire, and one sat upon each of them. And they were all filled with the Holy Spirit and began to speak with other tongues, as the Spirit gave them utterance. And there were dwelling in Jerusalem Jews, devout men, from every nation under heaven. And when this sound occurred, the multitude came together, and were confused, because everyone heard them speak in his own language. Then they were all amazed and marveled, saying to one another, "Look, are not all these who speak Galileans? And how is it that we hear, each in our own language in which we were born? Parthians and Medes and Elamites, those dwelling in Mesopotamia, Judea and Cappadocia, Pontus and Asia, Phrygia and Pamphylia, Egypt and the parts of Libya adjoining Cyrene, visitors from Rome, both Jews and proselytes, Cretans and Arabs—we hear them speaking in our own tongues the wonderful works of God" (Acts 2:1-11).

"For this reason a man shall leave his father and mother and be joined to his wife, and the two shall become one flesh." This is a great mystery, but I speak concerning Christ and the church (Ephesians 5:31-32).

THE MINISTRY OF THE SPIRIT

The Kingdom of God is expressed in the Bible in three different tenses. There is the *past tense* of the Kingdom, where God has been ruling the universe since the dawn of time (see Ps. 145:10-13). There is the *present tense*, which Jesus uses when He says that the Kingdom of God is *"within you,"* or is *"at hand"* (Luke 17:21; Matt. 10:7). Then there is the *future tense*, when the Kingdom of God will come to earth, finally putting down the revolt against His authority and forever establishing His will on earth as it is done in Heaven (see Luke 22:16-18; Matt. 25:31-36).

This is important to understand because many people see the Kingdom in only one tense. When Israel rejected its King, the King went into exile, so to speak, taking His Kingdom with Him, to come again another day not as a lamb silently led to the slaughter, but as the Lion of Judah, roaring in all His strength. When He does, He will bring down the enemy that first caused a war of rebellion to break out in the world. Then we will see the Kingdom in its fullness, in all its power and all its glory.

Some people believe that the Kingdom, because it was rejected in the first century, only has one tense—the *future* tense. Because of that, they think that the Kingdom was replaced by the Church.

But if you read Matthew 16, which is the first time Jesus used the word *church*, you find that He never put the Church on equal footing with the Kingdom. When Jesus asked Peter who He was, Peter said, *"You are the Christ, the Son of the living God"* (Matt. 16:16). To which Jesus responded:

Blessed are you, Simon Bar-Jonah, for flesh and blood has not revealed this to you, but My Father who is in heaven. And I also say to you *that you are Peter, and on this rock I will build **My church** and the gates of Hades shall not prevail against it* (Matthew 16:17-18).

It is interesting to note that after Christ's first mention of the word *church,* He uses the word *kingdom.* As a now-vanquishing King, Jesus passes His authority on to the next in command, so to speak. To Peter He says:

I will give you the keys of the kingdom of heaven, and whatever you bind on earth will be bound in heaven, and whatever you shall loose on earth will be loosed in heaven (Matthew 16:19).

E. Stanley Jones laments the historical consequences of both the Church's and Israel's failure to understand the Kingdom and their relationship to it:

The Church has lost the Kingdom of God. Call the roll of the tragedies in history, and they all root in the loss of that Kingdom. Take Israel, when it was said to her: *"The Kingdom of God will be taken away from you and given to a nation producing the fruits of it"* (Matt. 21:43 RSV). That refusal on the part of Israel began the long tragedy of a frustrated nation. Take the Crusades—men of violence tried to take that kingdom by force and succeeded in laying the foundations of hate and conflict through the centuries.[1]

Probably the best way to understand the relationship between the Church and the Kingdom is to see the Kingdom of God as a great empire beyond the sea, whose land, on this side of the sea, was seized millennia ago and is now occupied by rebel forces. The Church is something like an outpost to that empire. It exists in enemy-held territory. It exists to train soldiers and to equip them for spiritual warfare. It exists to teach these soldiers how to fight with weapons that are especially designed for that warfare, such as prayer. The outpost nourishes the recruits, caring for its sick, helping up its fallen, binding up its wounded.

Here is how we are trained to fight the spiritual war that wages all around us. We are taught to love our enemies, to pray for those who persecute us, to bless those who curse us, to forgive those who have hurt us.

A radical way of warfare. But that is God's strategy—to make us such beautiful people that the world will be wooed into His Kingdom.

Here is where we get the power to live such lives.

Keys.

Keys are a collective image of power and authority. Those who have the keys to the castle of a king, for example, can access any part of it, from the front door to the back door, from the pantry to the treasury. Those who have been given *"the keys of the kingdom of heaven"* have access to the castle of the King of kings, which is another way of saying that they have the power and authority of Heaven over things in the spiritual realm. Look at Matthew 10:1 and you will see how Jesus gave the disciples authority over unclean spirits and over every kind of disease. That is what is meant by the image of the key. And on that key ring is the all-important master key, which Jones uses as an exhortation to the Church collectively, as well as to you and me individually.

> If you have the key of the Kingdom, you find it a master-key, the key to live now and hereafter, life individual and collective…. So for the Church to be relevant the answer is simple: Discover the Kingdom, surrender to the Kingdom, make the Kingdom your life loyalty and your life program; then in everything and everywhere you will be relevant. For the Kingdom of God is relevancy—ultimate and final relevancy and when you have it, and it has you, then you are relevancy itself.

> Without the Kingdom the Church is irrelevant, except marginally. With the Kingdom the Church is relevant centrally and marginally—by its very nature it is relevant.

That is the key which the Church and its members desperately need if they are to represent heaven on earth, not in a *woeful* way, as has been our infamous past, but in a *wooful* way, which is the only way to a glorious future.[2]

The night before Jesus was forced into exile, He told His disciples it was to their advantage that He left, because only then could the Holy Spirit come (see John 16:7). The Spirit is the One who oversees these outposts we have come to know as the Church. He constructs these outposts, Paul tells us, distributes gifts to the soldiers, guides them, encourages them, equips them, and empowers them (see Rom. 12; 1 Cor. 12; Eph. 4). Jesus' final words to His disciples were about the Holy Spirit. He speaks to them as a departing general, giving final instructions for the troops He is leaving behind to continue the fight.

> *And being assembled together with them, He commanded them not to depart from Jerusalem, but to wait for the Promise of the Father, "which," He said, "you have heard from Me; for John truly baptized with water, but* **you shall be baptized with the Holy Spirit not many days from now.** *" Therefore, when they had come together, they asked Him, saying, "Lord, will You at this time restore the kingdom to Israel?" And He said to them, "It is not for you to know times or seasons which the Father has put in His own authority. But* **you shall receive power when the Holy Spirit has come upon you;** *and you shall be witnesses to Me in Jerusalem, and in all Judea and Samaria, and to the end of the earth"* (Acts 1:4-8).

When the Spirit came, He came to empower and embolden the King's soldiers, who were weary and on the verge of defeat. He came, Luke tells us in Acts 2, with fire and wind. Fire is symbolic of passion; wind is symbolic of power. And that is exactly how the Spirit ministered to the King's soldiers. When they came out of the upper room, they came out with passion and with power. Soon a crowd gathered, and the very man who had buckled under the peer pressure of three people around a campfire stood up and gave the most impassioned speech of his life. So powerful were his words that 3,000 people changed alliances and joined this fledgling fighting force.

This was not only Peter's experience but the experience of all the disciples, as Colin Urquhart notes in his book, *The Positive Kingdom:*

No longer were they the fearful men meeting secretly for fear of the Jews. Now they are men of the Spirit, given by God to water the seed of the Kingdom planted in them. So they pray: *"Enable your servants to speak Your word with great bold- ness. Stretch out Your hand to heal and perform miraculous signs and wonders through the name of Your holy servant Jesus"* (Acts 4:29-30).

They had been before the council for their boldness; they had recognized their need for greater boldness. They had seen great healings, still they prayed for God to stretch out His hand to heal. They were moving in the dimension of the miraculous; they asked for more in the name of Jesus.

And how does God answer such prayer? *"After they prayed, the place where they were meeting was shaken. And they were all filled with the Holy Spirit and spoke the word of God boldly"* (Acts 4:31). They had another Pentecost. God knew their need was to be filled with the Holy Spirit again. That was not to deny the value and validity of their former experience. They were learning that as Kingdom men with the commission to extend the Kingdom of God on earth, they were going to need constant empowering by the Holy Spirit.[3]

Before Jesus left, He told His disciples that they were to continue the battle for people's hearts, preaching the good news of the Kingdom— healing the sick, casting out demons, and raising the dead. In fact, He told them that they would do *even greater* works than He did, because He was going to the Father to intercede for them (see John 14:12). That promise was not only an encouragement for Jesus' followers in the first century but also for each and every one of us who is following Jesus in the twenty-first century.

As one of those following Jesus today, I want to report how the battle is faring on the front lines. The Holy Spirit is on the move, and the people of God are living beautiful lives, brimming with love and spilling joy everywhere they go. Territory that has been held by the enemy for millennia is being taken back. The blind see; the deaf hear; the lame walk; the dead are being raised; and the demons are in retreat.

Light is driving out darkness. Love is rooting out hate.

In Tanzania, Africa, I saw the Holy Spirit releasing the love of God over some 12,000 people. In one meeting, a rushing wind came into the meeting, and suddenly, the blind could see; the deaf could hear. What happened? The Kingdom had come near, and the King, in all His love, all His compassion, all His mercy, moved through the crowd in a mighty way.

In Kilimanjaro, Africa, 3,000 people showed up, hoping that Jesus would also show up. I asked the people to hold hands and just say "Papa" in Swahili, which is the word *Baba*. Probably 2,900 of the 3,000 were sick. Some had tumors. Others had goiters. Still others were paralyzed. There was a lot of witchcraft among the people, and the darkness was overwhelming. But each time they said "Baba," Heaven came down, like a splash of sunshine spilling out through an opening in a dark, cloud-covered sky. And suddenly, everything was new again. "Baba!" they cried out, over and over again, each time with more passion. After four or five times of calling His name, the love of God came down.

In the Philippines, God is at work in the communities of the poor, with the Holy Spirit wooing people into the Kingdom of God. Something so beautiful is happening there that people are drawn to be a part of it. It is not so much sermons that the Holy Spirit is using to draw people, but smiles. It is not lectures on love but demonstrations of love that are changing hearts.

Love is winning.

In China, the persecuted Church there is largely underground. They have nothing—no buildings, no budgets, no books. All they have is Jesus, and they are falling head over heels in love with Him.

Love is winning there, too.

In Asia, there is no Christian television, no books about God, no sermons on CDs, but they are so full of the Holy Spirit that it brings tears to my eyes.

One place in particular stands out. I can't remember being in a darker place. Fifty thousand people showed up. I was just one person, but one person with the Holy Spirit inside you changes the odds. The whole environment changed. Through some great oration I gave? No. Through the love I brought with me. And from the dove that lives inside me, beating its wings against my rib cage, so eager to get out and hover over the crowd, fanning them with the love of God.

And finally, Lahore, Pakistan. I was in a restaurant there, and the people behind the counter glared at me. But the Holy Spirit had my back. One man got up and left, and then suddenly the Holy Spirit fell on everyone there, and people were on the floor, weeping. Later, the owner of the restaurant came to my table. He asked me what had happened. I told him about the Holy Spirit and the love of God.

Here is what I *long* for you to know, what I *ache* for you to embrace.

The Kingdom of God is at hand!

This is the most exciting time in the world to be alive! It is not a time to be fearful; it is a time to be joyful!

In Romans 14:17, Paul says, *"the kingdom of God is not eating and drinking, but righteousness and peace and joy in the Holy Spirit."* The battle being waged is one where the *joy* of the Holy Spirit is bringing peace and righteousness to people's lives. I've been spreading that joy and peace for years, and only now am I beginning to learn the ways of the Spirit. As I told you before, I have always been a person to lean into things and lead from a place of my own strength. Now I am learning how to lean back and let the Holy Spirit do what He does best, which is changing people's hearts, miraculously and powerfully. In Acts 1:8, when Jesus tells His disciples to wait for the Spirit to empower them before they go into the world, the Greek word for power is *dunamis,* which is where we get our word *dynamite.*

Peter Kreeft, in his book, *The God Who Loves You,* explains how that dynamite gets inside of us.

> We are now in the age of the church or in the age of the Holy Spirit. Christ is still with us but not in the same form. His human body is in heaven, but His Spirit still groans over the face of the waters of our darkness and sin here on earth. The coming of the Holy Spirit is also love. In fact, it is a deepening of love, for it draws God into even greater intimacy with us. Love seeks above all intimacy, oneness, insideness with the beloved. The human body of Jesus is external to us. It is separated from us by time and space, whether we were His contemporaries on earth or whether we have been born centuries later. But His Spirit is not external but internal....
>
> Look at it this way. The Father is God outside you. The Son is God beside you. The Spirit is God inside you. Once God is inside you, you are spiritual dynamite.
>
> What is that dynamite? What turned the world upside down at Pentecost? What made saints saints? What makes the cynical, skeptical world turn its head at a Mother Teresa? What made the hard-nosed Roman Empire convert to the religion of a crucified Jewish carpenter? The world did not say, "See

how they explain one another!" but "See how they *love* one another!"[4]

How do you fight that kind of love?

You can't. Love wins. Love *always* wins. It is the way God has chosen to engage His enemies, and it is the way the Holy Spirit teaches *us* to engage ours.

THE MYSTERY OF THE CHURCH

The Church is a group of people literally "called out" from the world and formed into a new community. This new community allowed believing Gentiles to come together under one roof and worship with believing Jews—a radical idea at the time. Paul tells us that this mystery was revealed only after the partial hardening of Israel (see Rom. 11:25-32).

The mystery goes deeper. Not only were Jews accepting Gentiles as equals, but the rich were accepting the poor. Free men were accepting slaves. Men were accepting women. These ideas countered the social mores that existed both in the Jewish culture and in the Gentile culture. The Church was completely counter-cultural.

John Stott describes the difference in his insightful commentary on the Sermon on the Mount:

> Jesus emphasized that His true followers, the citizens of God's kingdom, were to be entirely different from others. They were not to take their cue from people around them, but from Him, and so prove to be genuine children of their heavenly Father.... Their character was to be completely distinct from what was admired by the world (the beatitudes). They were to shine like lights in the prevailing darkness. Their righteousness was to exceed that of the scribes and Pharisees, both in ethical behavior and in religious devotion, while their love was to

be greater and their ambition nobler than those of their pagan neighbors.[5]

What is the upside-down logic of this strategy? Jesus wanted His followers to be different from the world. He wanted them to think differently, speak differently, live differently. He wanted the world to see them as reflections of Himself. He wanted His followers to be so beautiful, so loving, so full of joy, that the world would be wooed by them.

That is what He has destined for us. But an even *greater* destiny awaits us.

There are many images used in the New Testament to describe this emerging group of radicals known as the Church. It is referred to as the *family* of God, a *Body* of believers, and the *Bride* of Christ, which, to me, is the most compelling image.

In several places in the Gospels, Jesus refers to Himself as a groom, both in parable (see Matt. 25:1-13) and in plain language (see Matt. 9:15). In the upper room—when Jesus told the disciples that He was going to prepare a place for them, to receive them to Himself, that where He is they might be also—the image Jesus uses is of a groom preparing the honeymoon suite for his bride (see John 14:2-3). In Ephesians, Paul talks about the relationship between a husband and a wife, then concludes his comments with these words: *"This mystery is great; but I am speaking with reference to Christ and the church"* (Eph. 5:32 NASB). In Ephesians 5:25-27, he underscores the analogy:

> *Christ also loved the church and gave Himself up for her, so that He might sanctify her, having cleansed her by the washing of water with the word, that He might present to Himself the church in all her glory, having no spot or wrinkle or any such thing; but that she would be holy and blameless* (NASB).

Finally, in the Book of Revelation, John records a scene in Heaven, where the voices of a great multitude call out:

"Let us rejoice and be glad and give the glory to Him, for the marriage of the Lamb has come and His bride has made herself ready." *It was given to her to clothe herself in fine linen, bright and clean; for the fine linen is the righteous acts of the saints* (Revelation 19:7-8 NASB).

In his book, titled *Heaven*, Randy Alcorn comments on this passage:

Her wedding dress is woven through her many acts of faithfulness while away from her Bridegroom on the fallen Earth. The picture is completely compelling. Each prayer, each gift, each hour of fasting, each kindness to the needy, all of these are the threads that have been woven together into this wedding dress. Her works have been empowered by the Spirit, and she has spent her life on Earth sewing her wedding dress for the day when she will be joined to her beloved Bridegroom.[6]

That is our destiny, and the role of the Holy Spirit is to prepare us for that destiny. His job? To make us fit for the King.

If you are married, I want you to think back for a moment. Remember your wedding day? How you started getting ready *months* before the wedding, losing weight, getting in shape, getting tan. Then, as the wedding day drew nearer, picking out your gown, your hairstyle. The day before the wedding, you were getting a facial, a manicure, pedicure, everything you can do to prepare yourself for the big day. Then it came. You woke up excited but nervous—so much to do, so little time left to do it all. But it all got done, and you're at the church now. Everyone's waiting in front. You're standing in your wedding dress, without spot or wrinkle. Every hair is in place. Your make up has been meticulously applied. Then the wedding march begins. Everyone stands, and you walk down the aisle. You have never felt more beautiful, more special, more loved.

Once at the altar, you look into the eyes of your beloved, and they are sparkling with joy. You see the delight in his smile, the love on his face. And you realize, all that joy, all that delight, all that love…is for me. *Me and only me!*

Now think about this. The Son of God has vowed Himself to you in the most sacred and intimate of ways. He has vowed to marry you—to live for all eternity wedded to *you*, to *me*, to all of us who make up His Church.

It sounds like a Cinderella story. Indeed, it is *the* quintessential Cinderella story.

You and the Prince of Peace at the ball, dancing together, holding each other, loving each other more with each passing day—sharing Paradise, together, forever.

Now think about this. *He* is the one who chose *you*. He's the one who first loved us all, loved us not because we were ravishing beauties with hearts of gold. No. That's not the picture the New Testament paints. He loved us, we are told, *while* we were yet sinners (see Rom. 5:8). That means He loved us in the moral equivalent to our being in rags and having ratty hair, with all our blemishes and belly fat, in all our selfishness and in all our indifference. When the Bible says that we love because Jesus first loved us (see 1 John 4:19), *that* is the person He first loved. Not the sweet, soft-spoken Cinderella in the fairy tale. It would be more like the Prince picking one of Cinderella's wicked, ugly step sisters, and saying, "She's the one. I want *her* to be my bride. I want *her* to share my throne, my fortune, my future."

How can this divine Bridegroom say to the human bride with all her blemishes and bad attitudes: "You are all fair, My love"?

Is God blind or just desperate?

He is neither. Because, as I said before, God sees our destiny, not our history. He looks forward, not backward. Maybe this example will help clarify how He can do this. There are two kinds of art forms: one is called a *sequential* art form; the other is called a *spatial* art form. It sounds technical, but it's really very simple. A sequential art form is something you experience in sequences, rather than all at one time. A movie, for example, is a sequential art form. You experience it a scene at a time, from beginning to end. A spatial art form is something you experience all at once. A painting, for example, is a spatial art form. You see it all at once.

As human beings, we experience life like a sequential art form: one day after another; one week, then another; one month, the next month. And so forth, from beginning to end. We experience the present, we remember the past, but we have no idea how our story is going to end. God, on the other hand, who exists outside of time, experiences our story not like a sequential art form but like a spatial art form. He sees the beginning, the middle, and the ending all at the same time.

So, God could see the past of the woman at the well before she met Jesus, He could see her at the well when Jesus filled the emptiness of her heart with His love, and He could see how her life ended up after years of being loved like that by a Man like that. And it was a beautiful ending, I'm almost sure of it.

That is how God sees you. He looks beyond the promiscuity, or whatever your past might have been, and He sees how your life will end up after being loved for a lifetime by Jesus.

And it's a beautiful ending.

I'm *absolutely* sure of that!

One other thing I'm absolutely sure of.

You are going to be one breathtakingly beautiful bride!

THE READER'S PRAYER

Dear Father,

Thank You for someone so wonderful to love.

Thank You for Jesus.

Thank You for something so wonderful to live for.

Thank You for Your Kingdom.

Thank You for something so wonderful to share.

Thank You for Your Spirit.

It all seems too incredible to believe that all these wonderful things are mine.

It seems like some dreamy tale in a child's world of make-believe, that I am worthy of being loved by someone like Jesus, that I am worthy of being honored with citizenship in Your Kingdom, that I am worthy of being trusted in giving away all that I have so generously received from Your Spirit.

It is the stuff of fairy tales, the misty, half-remembered dream of every child, the shy, unspoken hope of every teenager, the deepest, most earnest prayer of every adult.

But it is not a fairy tale.

And when I wake from that sleep that some call death, I know that the dreams that I once dared to dream really do come true.

And the most charming Prince of all awaits me there.

Me, His all-fair love!

CHAPTER 11

SEEING THE RETURN OF THE KING WITH HIS UNSHAKABLE KINGDOM

Then Jesus went out and departed from the temple, and His disciples came up to show Him the buildings of the temple. And Jesus said to them, "Do you not see all these things? Assuredly, I say to you, not one stone shall be left here upon another, that shall not be thrown down." Now as He sat on the Mount of Olives, the disciples came to Him privately, saying, "Tell us, when will these things be? And what will be the sign of Your coming, and of the end of the age?" And Jesus answered and said to them: "Take heed that no one deceives you. For many will come in My name, saying, 'I am the Christ,' and will deceive many. And you will hear of wars and rumors of wars. See to it that you are not troubled; for all these things must come to pass, but the end is not yet. For nation will rise against nation, and kingdom against kingdom. And there will be famines, pestilences, and earthquakes in various places. All these are the beginning of sorrows"
(Matthew 24:1-8).

Now Jesus knew that they desired to ask Him, and He said to them, "Are you inquiring among yourselves about what I said, 'A little while, and you will not see Me; and again a little while, and you will see Me'? Most assuredly, I say to you that you will weep and lament, but the world will rejoice; and you will be sorrowful, but your sorrow will be turned into joy. A woman, when she is in labor, has sorrow because her hour has come; but as soon as she has given birth to the child, she no longer remembers the anguish, for joy that a human being has been born into the world. Therefore you now have sorrow; but I will see you again and your heart will rejoice, and your joy no one will take from you" (John 16:19-22).

THE RETURN OF THE KING

In the Olivet Discourse in Matthew 24, Jesus uses the metaphor of *"sorrows"* or *"birth pangs"* (NASB) to describe the events leading to the coming of Christ with His Kingdom. A more modern term for "birth pangs" is *contractions.* During labor, the baby is pushed through the birth canal by contractions from the muscles of the uterus. The contractions begin at the top of the uterus and move the baby through the birth canal until the head crowns. With a few, hard, final pushes, the baby exits the mother's body into the fullness of life—a whole new world of sound, color, feelings, growth, and discovery.

The image of birth pangs connotes two things. One, the closer the baby is to being born, the *harder* the contractions are. And two, the closer the baby is to being born, the *closer* the contractions are. So when Jesus says that these things you see happening are the *"beginning of birth pangs,"* He is saying that it is going to get a lot worse before it is going to get better. Like a good OB/GYN, Jesus describes what the woman will go through to give birth. But then, He tells her what is waiting for her at the end of her pain.

A baby!

And with the baby will come such joy that she will forget about all the pain she went through to give it birth.

I was with Jennifer when she delivered all four of our children. I had gone with her to all her Lamaze classes. We practiced breathing exercises; rather, *she* practiced breathing exercises. I just coached her when to breathe, when to push, when to stop pushing. I was well trained. I read the printed material, followed the teacher's instructions, went through the exercises. I was prepared, or so I thought. And Jennifer was prepared, or so she thought. But there is nothing that quite prepares you for the real thing. When her water broke, I took her to the hospital. A nurse gave her a pelvic exam to see how far she had dilated. Sure enough, she was in labor. After she was prepped for delivery, a nurse timed her contractions. And sure enough, just like the book said, the contractions were getting harder and closer together.

I held her hand, wiped her forehead with a washcloth, gave her ice chips to suck on, smiled, assured her. Men have nothing in their experience to identify with what a woman goes through to give birth. Passing a kidney stone the size of cinder block might be close. Hand-holding isn't going to help a lot, I can tell you that. Pain, tears, anxiety, moaning, screaming, displacement of your insides, and an eight-pound mass with fingernails and toenails that haven't been clipped in nine months passing through a narrow, tender birth canal, forcing itself out of a hole the size of a quarter. Well, you get the picture.

Then, the phase the book terms *transition*. It should be termed "the-most-excruciating-pain-you-can-imagine-will-seem-like-a-hang-nail-compared-to-this." It's ugly, believe me, and I was just the one watching it.

But then, with a loud groan and a final push, it's over. The umbilical cord is cut; the baby cries; the nurses cleans her, wraps her in a warm covering, and then places her on Jennifer's breast. Suddenly, miraculously, an anesthetizing calm comes over my wife. Tears brim her eyes, then spill. This time, though, they are not tears of pain but tears of joy. She is exhausted but exhilarated.

Jesus was right.

So what can we learn from the metaphor? Life on earth is going to go through some scary, convulsive, painful times of displacement. Economies will crumble. Nations will topple. Heaving earthquakes will level cities. Widespread famines will devastate populations. And this is just the beginning of the labor.

There is an interesting part of Matthew 24 that is often overlooked by commentators. The question the disciples asked wasn't, "What will be the *signs* of Your coming?" (plural). But rather, "What will be the *sign* of Your coming?" (singular). All the things Jesus describes are merely birth pains, but the moment you know the birth is coming is revealed later in the passage.

> *Then you will be handed over to be persecuted and put to death, and you will be hated by all nations because of Me. At that time many will turn away from the faith and will betray and hate each other, and many false prophets will appear and deceive many people. Because of the increase of wickedness, the love of most will grow cold, but he who stands firm to the end will be saved.* ***And this gospel of the kingdom will be preached in the whole world as a testimony to all nations, and then the end will come*** (Matthew 24:9-14 NIV).

The sign is that the good news of the Kingdom will permeate the entire world. The word translated "nations" is the Greek word, *ethnos*, from which we get the word *"ethnic."* What Jesus has in view here is "people groups." In Pakistan, for example, there are 463 people groups, all with different dialects, different accents, different ways of communicating. Here is the exciting thing: the Gospel of the Kingdom is not only going to cross regional, religious, and racial borders; it is going into every nomadic tribe, through every tumble-down village, and across every nuance of humankind.

Is that exciting, or what?

And we are going to be a part of it! We are going to bring the refreshing, life-giving love of God to all those dry and desolate places. It is not a time to bury our talent, as many did during the fearful frenzy fueled by the Y2K panic-mongers. It's not a time to withdraw your resources; it is a time to invest them. Invest your time, talent, and treasure in the Kingdom, and you will be a part of bringing Heaven to earth.

Something *supernatural*. Something *phenomenal*. Something *eternal*.

The best is yet to come!

THE UNSHAKABLE KINGDOM

Doubtless the world will be full of fear during this labor. Likely the Church will be, too. But is that why Jesus tells us what He does in Matthew 24? No. He tells us so that we will know what to expect so that we *won't* fear. It's just the natural process of birth, He is saying. Don't focus on the *process*, however painful. Focus on *what the process is producing*.

A *King* is coming, and He is coming with *His Kingdom*. It will come from Heaven to earth. As it comes, it will displace every power and principality that isn't of God. A whole lot of shakin' is going to go on, as the writer to the Hebrews describes.

> *See that you do not refuse Him who speaks. For if they did not escape who refused Him who spoke on earth, much more shall we not escape if we turn away from Him who speaks from heaven, whose voice then shook the earth; but now He has promised, saying, "Yet once more I shake not only the earth, but also heaven." Now this, "Yet once more," indicates the removal of those things that are being shaken, as of things that are made, that the things which cannot be shaken may remain. Therefore, since we are receiving a kingdom which cannot be shaken, let us have grace, by which we may serve God acceptably with reverence and godly fear. For our God is a consuming fire* (Hebrews 12:25-29).

If you have ever been in an earthquake, you know how scary it is. Everything, and I mean everything, shakes. And you don't know how long the shaking is going to last or how hard it is going to get. That is one kind of shaking—a destructive shaking, where everything is toppled and turned to rubble. But there is another kind of shaking. It's the kind of shaking where an artist pours molten metal into an earthenware mold whose internal shape is a beautiful sculpture. Then, when the metal cools, he taps the mold with a hammer and shakes loose all that is stubbornly clinging to the artwork until only the statue remains.

Imagine God shaking you; He is doing it to remove everything that isn't love, isn't joy, isn't peace, isn't kindness, isn't—in a word—Jesus. The shaking may feel like you are being destroyed. In truth, you are being revealed. Through the hands of the artist, you are being restored to your original glory—not simply to the image of God that was defaced in the Fall, but to the image of Christ, in all its beauty, glory, and splendor.

If you knew that when the shaking began, would you be filled with fear of what you were losing, or would you be filled with love of what you were gaining?

John tells us that love casts out fear (see 1 John 4:18), and that is what Jesus is trying to tell us in Matthew 24 and John 16. The corollary, tragically, is also true—fear casts out love. When I was a child I saw several films on the end times, the rapture, the great tribulation. One was called *The Thief in the Night,* and it terrified me with a covers-over-my-face, pillow-over-my-head, frozen-in-a-fetal-position terror. I was a child, of course, full of childish fears, and part of that fear was that I didn't know who I was. Was I going to be left behind, hiding under my covers as the world caved in around me? Or would I go and my parents be left behind? What about my brother, my sister?

Fear is a terrible thing to live with, whether in a child or in an adult. Part of that fear is removed when we realize who we are, who we *really* are.

YOUR BORN IDENTITY

The Bourne Identity is a spy film based on Robert Ludlum's novel of the same name. The main character, Jason Bourne, is played by actor Matt Damon, who has suffered from *selective disassociated disorder,* a clinical term that describes people who have experienced trauma that has left them with a significant but not a total lapse of memory.

This man without a memory is found in the choppy waters of the Mediterranean, floating face-up at night in a wet suit off the coast of Marseille. An Italian fishing vessel picks him up, and one of the men takes two bullets out of his back, along with a laser device in his hip that reveals an account number to a Zurich bank.

As he recovers, the man can remember how to read, how to speak several foreign languages, how to tie knots. But he can't remember who he is, where he is from, or virtually anything from his past.

He arrives at Zurich one snowy night, and he finds rest on a park bench. Two policemen nudge him awake, questioning him. He cooperates until one of the men pokes a night stick into his chest. He freezes, then some instinctive reaction from his training kicks in. With lightning moves, he takes the night stick, pummels them both, leaving them sprawled on the snow, unconscious. Somehow he has managed to get one of their guns, and when he comes to himself, he is standing there, pointing it at them. He checks the gun, strips it of its magazine, throws both down, then sprints into the darkness.

The next day he enters the bank, accessing the safety deposit box that was coded to the laser device taken from his hip. In the box is a gun, thousands of dollars, and numerous passports, from which he learns his name is Jason Bourne. At the bank, he is recognized by surveillance cameras that reveal his identity to the clandestine branch of the government for which he works. In a daring escape—again, with reactions that are as instinctual as a cornered animal in the wild—he exits the building, unnoticed.

He manages to get a young woman to give him a ride to Paris, in hopes of finding some clue to his forgotten identity. Along the way she asks him what music he likes. He can't remember, he says, finally telling her he can't remember anything that happened before two weeks ago.

Bourne realizes he is being tracked down by someone who is out to kill him and has enlisted trained assassins to do it. He and the young woman, Marie, pull into a diner at night, and during their conversation, he says to her:

> I can tell you the license plate numbers of all six cars in the parking lot out front. I can tell you that the waitress is left-handed and the guy at the counter weighs 215 pounds and knows how to handle himself. I know that the best place to look for a gun is the cab of the grey car outside. I know that at this altitude I can run flat out for half a mile without my hand shaking...How do I know all that? How can I know all that and not know who I am?[1]

Times are coming—and in some parts of the world have already come—when followers of Jesus will face the persecution He describes in the Olivet Discourse: *"Then they will deliver you up to tribulation and kill you, and you will be hated by all nations for My name's sake"* (Matt. 24:9).

If we are to be prepared for such times, we have to know our identity—our "born identity." Not the identity we get from our physical genealogy but the identity we get from our spiritual genealogy (see John 3:1-8).

We are children of the King—beloved sons and daughters, the delight of His heart, the apple of His eye. But we not only have to know who we are, we have to know *why* we are here. We are here to reflect the heart of the King, and, in doing so, we will represent the winsome beauty of His Kingdom in every area of our lives so that His Kingdom comes and His will is done on earth as it is in Heaven.

When we face opposition and people hate us, persecute us, curse us, and harm us, we are to respond by loving those who hate us, praying for those who persecute us, blessing those who curse us, and forgiving those who harm us. And we are to do it instinctively—not in the way Jason Bourne did, but in the way Jesus Christ did, *"who, when He was reviled, did not revile in return; when He suffered, He did not threaten, but committed Himself to Him who judges righteously"* (1 Pet. 2:23)

How do we learn to do those things, and to do them instinctively? Ironically, the same way Jason Bourne did. He was trained. He had book training and classroom training. He had an instructor who walked him through life-threatening situations so he would know how to react, quickly and decisively. He was also put through exercises in hand-to-hand combat.

For us to have the equivalent training in the spiritual realm, we must have training in the Word and teaching at church and at conferences. We must have a mentor to show us the skills of the heart. And, in order to respond to the larger conflicts in life, we must start by mastering the smaller conflicts.

Consider the supervisor at work, for example, who pummels you at every performance review; he is not an enemy, but from time to time acts like one. The Word gives clear instructions how to respond to such a person:

> *Servants, be submissive to your masters with all fear, not only to the good and gentle, but also to the harsh. For this is commendable, if because of conscience toward God one endures grief, suffering wrongfully. For what credit is it if, when you are beaten for your faults, you take it patiently? But when you do good and suffer, if you take it patiently, this is commendable before God. For to this you were called, because Christ also suffered for us, leaving us an example, that you should follow His steps* (1 Peter 2:18-21).

Perhaps you have an antagonistic mate, for another example, who criticizes you, even curses you. Again, the mate is not the enemy, but from time to time can function as one. How do you respond? The Word is our training manual, instructing us to respond to the person not in kind but in kindness, not returning insult for insult but giving a blessing instead (see Luke 6:27-38).

Or maybe a friend hurts you, angers you, and you start the needling work of embroidering a monologue to tell the person off. Here is what our mentor, Paul, would say to that:

Let all bitterness, wrath, anger, clamor, and evil speaking be put away from you, with all malice. And be kind to one another, tenderhearted, forgiving one another, even as God in Christ forgave you (Ephesians 4:31-32).

This is how light dispels darkness, how love defeats hate. It is not a battle fought with guns and bombs or even diplomacy because it is a *spiritual* battle, not a physical one. Prayer is one of the spiritual weapons that Paul says we are equipped with in Ephesians 6:

*Finally, my brethren, be strong in the Lord and in the power of His might. Put on the whole armor of God, that you may be able to stand against the wiles of the devil. For we do not wrestle against flesh and blood, but against principalities, against powers, against the rulers of the darkness of this age, against spiritual hosts of wickedness in the heavenly places. Therefore take up the whole armor of God, that you may be able to withstand in the evil day, and having done all, to stand. Stand therefore, having girded your waist with truth, having put on the breastplate of righteousness, and having shod your feet with the preparation of the gospel of peace; above all, taking the shield of faith with which you will be able to quench all the fiery darts of the wicked one. And take the helmet of salvation, and the sword of the Spirit, which is the word of God; **praying always with all prayer and supplication in the Spirit, being watchful to this end with all perseverance and supplication*** *for all the saints*—*and for me, that utterance may be given to me, that I may open my mouth boldly to make known the mystery of the gospel, for which I am an ambassador in chains; that in it I may speak boldly, as I ought to speak* (Ephesians 6:10-20).

Paul got this example from the King Himself. When Jesus was in the upper room the night in which He was betrayed, He told Peter that satan had demanded permission to sift him like wheat. *"But I have prayed for you,"* Jesus assured him, *"that your faith should not fail"* (Luke 22:31-32). And, when Jesus was dying on the Cross, He pleaded with the Father that this sin would not be held against those who played a part in putting Him there (see Luke 23:34).

This is how we should be training now, faithful in the lesser persecutions that come our way so that we will be ready for the greater ones.

Your "born identity" is your truest self which shares the same spiritual DNA as Jesus. Never forget who you are, and you will never forget why you are here. Never forget why you are here, and you will never forget what to do, especially in difficult times.

From time to time we all forget. Even I forget sometimes. When that happens, I pray the Holy Spirit whispers to your spirit:

Remember who you are.

Remember why you are here.

And everything you need to say or do will come back to you.

Instinctively.

THE READER'S PRAYER

Dear Heavenly Father,

Thank you for the words of our mentor, the apostle Paul. As I pray through them, replace my fear of going through a painful birth and help me to focus on my love for the wonderful baby that is going to be birthed.

I consider that the sufferings of this present time are not worthy to be compared with the glory which shall be revealed in us. For the earnest expectation of the creation eagerly waits for the revealing of the sons of God. For the creation was subjected to futility, not willingly, but because of Him who subjected it in hope; because the creation itself also will be delivered from the bondage of corruption into the glorious liberty of the children of God.

For we know that the whole creation groans and labors with birth pangs together until now. Not only that, but we also who have the firstfruits of the Spirit, even we ourselves groan within ourselves, eagerly waiting for the adoption, the redemption of our body.

For we were saved in this hope, but hope that is seen is not hope; for why does one still hope for what he sees? But if we hope for what we do not see, we eagerly wait for it with perseverance.

Likewise the Spirit also helps in our weaknesses. For we do not know what we should pray for as we ought, but the Spirit Himself makes intercession for us with groanings which cannot be uttered. Now He who searches the hearts knows what the mind of the Spirit is, because He makes intercession for the saints according to the will of God.

And we know that all things work together for good to those who love God, to those who are the called according to His purpose. For whom He foreknew, He also predestined to be conformed to the image of His Son, that He might be the firstborn among many brethren.

Moreover whom He predestined, these He also called; whom He called, these He also justified; and whom He justified, these He also glorified.

What then shall we say to these things? If God is for us, who can be against us?

He who did not spare His own Son, but delivered Him up for us all, how shall He not with Him also freely give us all things? Who shall bring a charge against God's elect? It is God who justifies. Who is he who condemns? It is Christ who died, and furthermore is also risen, who is even at the right hand of God, who also makes intercession for us.

Who shall separate us from the love of Christ? Shall tribulation, or distress, or persecution, or famine, or nakedness, or peril, or sword? As it is written:

"For Your sake we are killed all day long; we are accounted as sheep for the slaughter."

Yet in all these things we are more than conquerors through Him who loved us.

For I am persuaded that neither death nor life, nor angels nor principalities nor powers, nor things present nor things to come, nor height nor depth, nor any other created thing, shall be able to separate us from the love of God which is in Christ Jesus our Lord (Romans 8:18-39).

Amen.

CHAPTER 12

SEEING PARADISE RESTORED
AND HUMANITY REDEEMED

Eye has not seen, nor ear heard, nor have entered into the heart of man the things which God has prepared for those who love Him (1 Corinthians 2:9).

The Bible is the story of God establishing His rule on earth so that His Kingdom could come and His will would be done on earth as it is in Heaven.

The story begins in Genesis and ends in Revelation. It begins in a garden and ends in a garden. It begins in Paradise and ends in Paradise. It begins with a Tree of Life and ends with a Tree of Life. It begins with a family and ends with a family. It begins with the rule of God and ends with the rule of God.

Between the once-upon-a-time beginning, though, and the happily-ever-after ending, Paradise is lost. The earth falls under a curse. And the whole world lies under the power of the evil one.

Like Narnia.

C.S. Lewis' epic tale, *The Lion, the Witch and the Wardrobe* from his *Chronicles of Narnia*, is the story of paradise lost and paradise restored. In the story, Aslan the lion is rightful king of Narnia, but the White Witch has taken over his domain. Once pristine in its innocence and lush in its beauty, Narnia falls under her spell, becoming a place where it is always winter but never Christmas.

Treachery, lies, greed, and intimidation fill the land. A blanket of snow covers everything, including the Narnians the White Witch has turned into stone statues. The witch's spies are everywhere, and everyone lives in fear.

But the stories of the old Narnia live on in the people's hearts—stories of the time when Aslan ruled and there was joy and laughter, the land was fruitful and fragrant, and peace reigned unopposed. All eagerly await his return.

There are sightings of him here and there, fleeting glimpses, brief encounters. Aslan makes stealthy forays into the land, and everywhere he steps, the snow melts. In his footprints, little patches of life emerge. Tufts of grass and flowers. Little Edens, so to speak.

That is an apt picture of the world that you and I are living in. It, too, is under a spell. It, too, lies under the power of the evil one. So much life lies dormant, awaiting the warmth of the sun and the renewal of spring. But it is so cold in so many parts of the world, and snow seems to cover everything, where it is always winter and never Christmas.

I can tell you from my travels around the world that Aslan is on the move. And everywhere He steps, little Edens emerge: a human heart thaws, sprigs of life spring up, and so many seeds that have lain dormant for millennia germinate and take root.

I've seen His footsteps in foreign lands. I've seen small gardens springing up, bearing fruit. I've seen individuals come to life. I've seen marriages and families come to life. I've seen paradise restored in villages, towns, cities. One day soon, I believe we will see entire nations and people groups redeemed.

Aslan is on the move! Heaven is opening up. His Kingdom is coming down. One day He will come with the Kingdom, the power, and the glory that is His. All the earth will bow before Him, and in His presence it will blush into a beauty that is beyond imagining.

Paradise *will be* restored. See for yourself.

Now I saw a new heaven and a new earth, for the first heaven and the first earth had passed away. Also there was no more sea. Then I, John, saw the holy city, New Jerusalem, coming down out of heaven from God, prepared as a bride adorned for her husband. And I heard a loud voice from heaven saying, "Behold, the tabernacle of God is with men, and He will dwell with them, and they shall be His people. God Himself will be with them and be their God. And God will wipe away every tear from their eyes; there shall be no more death, nor sorrow, nor crying. There shall be no more pain, for the former things have passed away." Then He who sat on the throne said, "Behold, I make all things new" (Revelation 21:1-5a).

Think of it. There will no longer be any poverty or plagues, sin or shame, hateful words or horrendous wars. There will no longer be any tears—no pain, no migraines, no cancer, no heart disease, no sorrows of any kind. There will no longer be any death—flowers will not wither, nor will faces; leaves will not wilt, nor will limbs. There will no longer be any curse—no thorns, no thistles, no resistance whatsoever. It will no longer be a dog-eat-dog world, but rather a world where the wolf will dwell with the lamb, the leopard will lie down with the goat, the lion will eat straw like the ox, the nursing child will play by the hole of a cobra, and they will not hurt each other or destroy each other (see Isa. 11:6-9).

As I told you before, Jesus has a special place in His heart for children. Because of that, children have a special place not only in our hearts but in our conferences. Many of them have had incredible experiences with the Holy Spirit. Some of them tell remarkable stories of visiting Heaven.

A recently published book, *Heaven Is for Real,* tells the story of a boy, not yet four years old, who, during an appendectomy, went to Heaven. His name is Colton. His memories are not only vivid but verifiable in the Bible. His father recounts some of the stories:

> I smoothed Colton's blanket across his chest and tucked him in snug the way he liked—and for the first time since he started talking about heaven, I intentionally tried to trip him up. "I remember you saying you stayed with Pop," I said. "So when it got dark and you went home with Pop, what did you two do?"

> Suddenly serious, Colton scowled at me. "It doesn't get dark in heaven, Dad! Who told you *that?*"

> I held my ground. "What do you mean it doesn't get dark?"

> "God and Jesus light up heaven. It never gets dark. It's always bright."[1]

The passage from Revelation 21:23 came back to his dad: *"The city had no need of the sun or of the moon to shine in it, for the glory of God illuminated it. The Lamb is its light"* (see also Rev. 22:5).

In 2003 and 2004, Colton seemed to fixate on certain things. Fragments of his memories fell out at the dinner table, in the car, at night as he was tucked into bed. He told his parents he saw gates in Heaven. "They were made of gold and there were pearls on them," he said.[2] Again, the description was remarkably similar to the one in Revelation: *"The twelve gates were twelve pearls: each individual gate was of one pearl. And the street of the city was pure gold, like transparent glass"* (Rev. 21:21).

Then Colton talked about the holy city being made of something shiny, like gold or silver. He talked about how beautiful the flowers were, and how there were animals everywhere. Again, his descriptions lined up remarkably with Scripture.

And he carried me away in the Spirit to a great and high mountain, and showed me the great city, the holy Jerusalem, descending out of heaven from God, having the glory of God. Her light was like a most precious stone, like a jasper stone, clear as crystal. Also she had a great and high wall with twelve gates, and twelve angels at the gates, and names written on them, which are the names of the twelve tribes of the children of Israel: three gates on the east, three gates on the north, three gates on the south, and three gates on the west. Now the wall of the city had twelve foundations, and on them were the names of the twelve apostles of the Lamb. And he who talked with me had a gold reed to measure the city, its gates, and its wall. The city is laid out as a square; its length is as great as its breadth. And he measured the city with the reed: twelve thousand furlongs. Its length, breadth, and height are equal. Then he measured its wall: one hundred and forty-four cubits, according to the measure of a man, that is, of an angel. The construction of its wall was of jasper; and the city was pure gold, like clear glass (Revelation 21:10-18).

Colton also chattered on about the rainbow of colors he saw there. Again, strikingly similar to the restored Paradise that John talks about:

The foundations of the wall of the city were adorned with all kinds of precious stones: the first foundation was jasper, the second sapphire, the third chalcedony, the fourth emerald, the fifth sardonyx, the sixth sardius, the seventh chrysolite, the eighth beryl, the ninth topaz, the tenth chrysoprase, the eleventh jacinth, and the twelfth amethyst (Revelation 21:19-20).

One thing the young boy remembered about our redeemed humanity bears repeating. "Dad, nobody's old in heaven," Colton said. "And nobody wears glasses."[3]

Frederick Buechner once said that the Gospel is part tragedy, part comedy, and part fairy tale. The tragedy—or bad news—is that we have all sinned and fallen short of the glory of God, and that the wages of sin is death (see Rom. 3:23; 6:23). The comedy—or good news—is that Jesus loved us while we were yet sinners and died for us so that we wouldn't have to (see Rom. 5:8). The fairy tale—or the too-good-to-be-true news—is that God not only *accepts* us, He *perfects* us. He transforms us from sinners to saints, like the transformations in fairy tales where the frog is transformed into a prince or the beast is transformed into someone beautiful.

Paradise will be restored. Humanity will be redeemed. One day light will overcome darkness, love will overcome hate, life will overcome death, and there will be joy throughout the universe. The evil one will be defeated along with death. Then there will be the biggest celebration the universe has ever seen. There will be a wedding, a banquet, a ball, music and dancing. And we will be just like Jesus, the Scriptures tell us (see Rom. 8:29). In the twinkling of an eye, we will be changed into His image (see 1 Cor. 15:42-58). John, who wrote so much of the restored Paradise, says this about our restoration:

> *Beloved, now we are children of God, and it has not appeared as yet what we will be. We know that when He appears, we will be like Him, because we will see Him just as He is* (1 John 3:2 NASB).

Can you even begin to imagine what you and I will be like? No longer will we have to struggle with sin. No longer will we even be tempted. No longer will we have to fight addictions or the addictions of those we love. Not only will the power of sin be defeated in our lives, the very presence of sin will be banished. Forever.

No wonder that Paul, who himself, like Colton, was taken up to Paradise, said that eye has not seen or ear heard all that God has prepared for those who love him (see 1 Cor. 2:9).

A Final Word

Thank you for taking this journey with me. I have loved having you as a companion along the way, loved sharing something of my journey to the heart of God. Traveling mercies for the road ahead, my friend. I would like to close with one more story that Colton's dad tells.

"Hey, Colton," I said, kneeling next to him, "when you were in heaven, did you ever see God's throne?"

Colton looked at me quizzically. "What's a throne, Daddy?"

I picked up the Bible storybook and pointed to the picture of Solomon seated in his court. "A throne is like the king's chair. It's the chair that only the king can sit in."

"Oh, yeah! I saw that a bunch of times!" Colton said.

My heart sped up a little. Was I really going to get a glimpse into the throne room of heaven? "Well, what did God's throne look like?"

"It was big, Dad...*really, really* big, because God is the biggest one there is. And he really, really loves us, Dad. You can't *belieeeve* how much he loves us!"[4]

Our God is really, really big. And He really, really does love us, you and me. You can't believe how much He loves us! If, by some impartation of faith, we *can* believe it, it will change the way we look at Him, the way we look at ourselves, the way we look at others, and the way we look at the future.

In a word, it will change *everything*.

And now, before I say goodbye, I would like to pray for you one last time.

Author's Prayer

Dear Papa,

*You **really, really** are a big God.*

*And You really, really **do** love us.*

I pray the reader of this book understands just how much.

I pray for an impartation of Your Spirit to give the person holding this book a baptism of love that lasts a lifetime.

Give this beloved son of Yours, or this beloved daughter, new eyes with which to see.

New eyes to see You.

New eyes to see herself, or himself.

New eyes to see other people.

And new eyes to see the future.

Wow! What a future! What a celebration!

And we are the guests of honor!

*It's for **us**—for the reader and for me and for all who have become like children, skipping into the Kingdom of God.*

Joy for the journey, Lord.

I pray for joy along the way to this magical Kingdom that You have prepared for all who love You.

Help us to love well and to live in the fearless and festive awareness that we are the children of the King.

It's in His precious name I pray.

Amen.

ENDNOTES

Epigraph

1. E. Stanley Jones, *The Unshakable Kingdom and the Unchanging Person* (Bellingham, WA: McNett Press, 1995), 38.

Part 1 Seeing God the Way Jesus Sees Him

1. Gregory A. Boyd, *Repenting of Religion: Turning From Judgment to the Love of God* (Grand Rapids, MI: Baker Books, 2004), 32.

Chapter 1 Seeing God in His Glory

1. The words are from Lord Darlington, a character in Oscar Wilde's play, *Lady Windermere's Fan*, Act III. The play was first performed at St. James' Theater in London on February 22, 1892; it was first published in London in 1893.

2. The material on astronomy, along with the illustration comparing sand to stars, is from Judy Cannato, *Radical Amazement: Contemplative Lessons from Black Holes, Supernovas, and Other Wonders of the Universe* (Notre Dame, IN: Sorin Books, 2006), 7-8.

3. Peter Kreeft, *Heaven, the Heart's Deepest Longing*, expanded ed. (San Francisco, CA: Ignatius Press, 1989), 118-119.

Chapter 2 Seeing the Culture of Heaven

1. C.S. Lewis, *Letters to Malcolm: Chiefly on Prayer* (San Diego, CA: Harcourt Brace & Co., 1992).

2. Ken Gire, *The Divine Embrace: An Invitation to the Dance of Intimacy with Christ, One Exhilarating, Ennobling, Uncertain Step at a Time* (Wheaton, IL: Tyndale House Publishers, 2003), 191.

3. Sydney Carter, "Lord of the Dance" (Carol Stream, IL: Stainer & Hall, Ltd., administered by Hope Publishing Co., 1963).

Chapter 3 Seeing God Through the Eyes of His Son

1. *Merriam Webster Online,* s.v. "Prodigal," accessed March 26, 2011, http://www.merriam-webster.com/dictionary/prodigal?show=0&t=1300167396.

Part 2 Seeing Ourselves the Way the Father Sees Us

1. Kreeft, *Heaven, the Heart's Deepest Longing,* 191.

Chapter 4 Seeing Man in His Glory and Paradise in Its Splendor

1. The material on the image of God is found in Ken Gire, *The Work of His Hands* (Ann Arbor, MI: Vine Books, 2002), from the chapter, "The Image of God."

2. Bill Johnson, *When Heaven Invades Earth* (Shippensburg, PA: Destiny Image Publishers, Inc., 2003), 30.

3. Abarim Publications, "Meaning and Etymology of the Hebrew Name Eden," Quantum Mechanics, Chaos Theory and the Reliability of the Bible, accessed March 26, 2011, http://www.abarim-publications.com/Meaning/Eden.html.

4. Richard Leary, "Frederick Law Olmsted," New Bedford Home Page, accessed March 26, 2011, http://www.newbedford.com/olmsted.html.

Chapter 5 Seeing Paradise Lost and Our Homesickness for Eden

1. For the material in this chapter that shows how love is behind the judgments of God, I am indebted to the teaching of Peter Kreeft in his book, *The God Who Loves You* (Ann Arbor, MI: Servant Books, 1992).

2. Boyd, *Repenting of Religion*, 109.

3. Jean Delumeau, *History of Paradise: The Garden of Eden in Myth and Tradition* (Urbana, IL: University of Illinois Press, 2000).

4. Ibid., 55.

5. C.S. Lewis, *The Problem of Pain* (New York, NY: MacMillan Co., 1962), 145.

Chapter 6 Seeing Ourselves as Beloved Sons and Daughters

1. Kreeft, *Heaven, the Heart's Deepest Longing*, 70.

2. Gregory A. Boyd, *Seeing Is Believing* (Grand Rapids, MI: Baker Books, 2004), 66.

3. The scene with Mr. Holland and his student is from *Mr. Holland's Opus*, 1995, from Interscope Communications and PolyGram Filmed Entertainment, directed by Stephen Herek, starring Richard Dreyfuss.

Part 3 Seeing Others the Way the Father Sees Them

1. Kreeft, *Heaven, the Heart's Deepest Longing*, 37.

Chapter 7 Seeing Humanity Through Heaven's Eyes

1. Sue Monk Kidd, *When the Heart Waits* (New York, NY: HarperOne, 1990), 4.

2. The story about John being criticized by one of his disciples is taken from Peter Kreeft, *The God Who Loves You,* 23.

3. Kidd, *When the Heart Waits,* 178-179.

Chapter 8 Seeing Jesus Through Heaven's Eyes

1. Jones, *The Unshakable Kingdom and the Unchanging Person,* 154-155.

2. Frederick Buechner, *The Magnificent Defeat* (San Francisco, CA: Harper & Row, 1985).

3. Colin Urquhart, *The Positive Kingdom* (London, UK: Hodder and Stoughton, 1985), 41-42.

4. Jones, *The Unshakable Kingdom,* 75.

5. Ibid., 13.

6. William Law, "William Law Quotes," BrainyQuote, accessed March 26, 2011, http://www.brainyquote.com/ quotes/authors/w/william_law.html.

7. Frederick Buechner, *The Clown in the Belfry* (San Francisco, CA: Harper San Francisco, 1992), 170.

8. Jones, *The Unshakable Kingdom,* 34.

9. Buechner, *The Clown in the Belfry,* 171.

Chapter 9 Seeing Your Enemies Through Heaven's Eyes

1. G.K. Chesterton quoted in Ken Gire's book, *Reflections on the Word* (Colorado Springs, CO: Chariot Victor Publishing, 1998), pp. 72-73.

2. Jones, *The Unshakable Kingdom and the Unchanging Person.*

3. Dietrich Bonhoeffer, *The Cost of Discipleship* (New York, NY: Macmillan Co., 1959).

4. Martin Luther King, Jr., *Strength to Love* (New York, NY: Harper & Row, 1963).

5. Ibid.

6. Abraham Lincoln, *Great Speeches* (New York, NY: Dover Publications, 1991), 107-108.

7. Souad, *Burned Alive: A Survivor of an "Honor Killing" Speaks Out* (New York, NY: Grand Central Publishing, 2004), 13.

8. Ibid., 29.

9. Ibid., 30.

10. Ibid., 48.

11. Ibid., 69.

12. Donald Miller, *A Million Miles in a Thousand Years* (Nashville, TN: Thomas Nelson, 2009), 117-118.

Part 4 Seeing the Future the Way the Father Sees It

1. Kreeft, *The God Who Loves You*, 20-21.

Chapter 10 Seeing the Ministry of the Spirit and the Mystery of the Church

1. Jones, *The Unshakable Kingdom and the Unchanging Person*, 18.

2. Ibid., 19.

3. Urquhart, *The Positive Kingdom*, 118-119.

4. Kreeft, *The God Who Loves You*, 109-110.

5. John Stott, *The Message of the Sermon on the Mount* (Downers Grove, IL: IVP, 1989).

6. Randy Alcorn, *Heaven* (Wheaton, IL: Tyndale House Publishers, 2004).

Chapter 11 Seeing the Return of the King With His Unshakable Kingdom

1. *The Bourne Identity.* Universal Studios, 2002. Adapted from Robert Ludlum's book of the same title. Screenwriters: Tony Gilroy and W. Blake Herron. Director: Doug Liman. Actor: Matt Damon.

Chapter 12 Seeing Paradise Restored and Humanity Redeemed

1. Todd Burpo with Lynn Vincent, *Heaven Is for Real* (Nashville, TN: Thomas Nelson, 2010), 104.

2. Ibid., 105.

3. Ibid., 121.

4. Ibid., 100.

ABOUT LEIF HETLAND

Leif Hetland was born in Stavanger, Norway. He is the president and founder of Global Mission Awareness and Leif Hetland Ministries. He has traveled in 76 countries and extensively in the U.S. motivating people to see the Kingdom of God on earth as it is in Heaven. He is a popular, sought-after speaker at conferences, churches, and ministries. He is married to Jennifer, and they have four amazing children.

Leif Hetland's website is:

www.globalmissionawareness.com

In the right hands, This Book will Change Lives!

Most of the people who need this message will not be looking for this book. To change their lives, you need to put a copy of this book in their hands.

> *But others (seeds) fell into good ground, and brought forth fruit, some a hundred-fold, some sixty-fold, some thirty-fold* (Matthew 13:8).

Our ministry is constantly seeking methods to find the good ground, the people who need this anointed message to change their lives. Will you help us reach these people?

> *Remember this—a farmer who plants only a few seeds will get a small crop. But the one who plants generously will get a generous crop* (2 Corinthians 9:6).

EXTEND THIS MINISTRY BY SOWING
3 BOOKS, 5 BOOKS, 10 BOOKS, **OR MORE TODAY,**
AND BECOME A LIFE CHANGER!

Thank you,

Don Nori Sr., Founder
Destiny Image
Since 1982

DESTINY IMAGE PUBLISHERS, INC.

"Speaking to the Purposes of God for This Generation
and for the Generations to Come."

VISIT OUR NEW SITE HOME AT
WWW.DESTINYIMAGE.COM

FREE SUBSCRIPTION TO DI NEWSLETTER

Receive free unpublished articles by top DI authors, exclusive

discounts, and free downloads from our best and newest books.

Visit www.destinyimage.com to subscribe.

Write to: Destiny Image
               P.O. Box 310
               Shippensburg, PA 17257-0310

Call: 1-800-722-6774

Email: orders@destinyimage.com

For a complete list of our titles or to place an order
online, visit www.destinyimage.com.